Advance Praise for *Management Experience Acquired*

"*Management Experience Acquired* captures the essential elements of management from the ground up, and provides practical advice for navigating the often turbulent waters of the workplace. The book not only contains the considerable wisdom that Wendy Powell has gained during a highly productive career advising supervisors and employees, it also provides practical examples that will empower individuals to handle real-world situations effectively.

Effective management is a delicate balancing act that requires alertness, technical skill, and artful action. In *Management Experience Acquired*, Wendy Powell simply and expertly outlines the key issues required to attain and sustain balance. The reader will enjoy meeting dozens of workplace 'Joes' who vividly portray real-world individuals commonly found in the workplace.

Successful management requires continuous learning and practice. This book provides a wealth of opportunity for learning and practice in a style that is both useful and fun. The book is terrific. The complex issues are outlined and explained simply. The workplace 'Joes' are a great way to tell the story and explain the concepts. Enjoy the experience!"
—John M. Toller, Chief Human Resources Officer at East Carolina University and past president of the College and University Professional Association for Human Resources

"This book is simply a pioneering masterpiece that paves the way for handling the new managerial requirements of today's corporate culture. A must-read for all those who want to succeed."
—Jose A. Velez, Executive Managing Partner at The Executive Diamond Group and former MBA student of Wendy Powell

"Wendy Powell's book is a no-nonsense, practical guide for managers wanting to create an effective partnership with employees. The book is down-to-earth, sensitive to the realities of leadership and followership, and contains interesting case studies. The Art Linkletter-like quotes from young people lighten the content and offer an untarnished view of our working world by children who will grow to experience what we have created as managers."
—Dr. Barbara Butterfield, Senior Consultant at Sibson Consulting, a division of The Segal Company, and past president of the College and University Professional Association for Human Resources

"I am both pleased and honored to recommend Wendy Powell's book. Having read the contents, I feel it contains a great deal of helpful information for executives of all ages. Being in the front offices for many years in the major leagues as an executive, this book would have assisted me in many ways. I recommend it!"
—Fred Ferreira, Former Vice President and Director of International Operations of the New York Yankees, Montreal Expos, and Florida Marlins

"Wendy Powell's *Management Experience Acquired* is a terrific resource for anyone tasked with the ongoing challenges of managing employees in today's dynamic workplace environment. Whether you are growing a small business or leading a major agency or corporation, this book will give you the necessary

strategies and techniques to maximize individual and organizational performance. Powell writes in an upbeat, lively style, with the overriding belief that people do matter, and serves as your personal HR coach and mentor every step of the way. This book should be kept within arm's reach. You'll refer to it often!"
—Dr. Andy Edelman, Founder and CEO of Spectrum Interactiv, Inc. and author of *When Words Fail: How to Defuse, Control and Resolve Conflicts and Confrontations in Any Setting or Situation*

"The management of a company's human resources is generally not a priority topic for most business executives. However, in these turbulent times, it has become critical to manage your investment in employees as closely as revenues, profits, and cash. Ms. Powell's guide provides clarity on achieving the most with your staff."
—Marc Gingold, President and CEO of Océ Financial Services, Inc.

"This book reads like a good conversation on management. Wendy writes as she teaches, reinforcing the common sense we all have. 'Joe' and Wendy share experiences and give examples that will help current and future managers succeed."
—ElizaBeth Kalmbach, former student of Wendy Powell

"I believe *Management Experience Acquired* should be compulsory reading for any first-time manager or manager striving to improve his or her managerial skills."
—Anthony Dyett, former MBA student of Wendy Powell

Management Experience ~~Required~~ *Acquired*

Necessary Skills
for Successfully
Managing Any
Employee

Wendy N. Powell

Management Experience Acquired: Necessary Skills for Successfully Managing Any Employee
Published by Synergy Books
P.O. Box 80107
Austin, Texas 78758

For more information about our books, please write us, e-mail us at info@synergybooks.net, or visit our web site at www.synergybooks.net.

Publisher's Cataloging-in-Publication
(Provided by Quality Books, Inc.)

Powell, Wendy N.
Management experience acquired : necessary skills for successfully managing any employee / Wendy N. Powell.
p. cm.
Includes bibliographical references and index.
LCCN 2009939670
ISBN-13: 978-0-9842358-2-7
ISBN-10: 0-9842358-2-5

1. Management. I. Title.

HD31.P69 2010 658
QBI09-600210

Please visit www.ManagementExperienceAcquired.com for more information.

10 9 8 7 6 5 4 3 2 1

Of course, to my husband Terry Powell and my son Ryan Powell, who have provided me with the love, support, and great ideas to complete this book, and to the rest of my family, including the ones in heaven.

To the wonderful managers I've had the pleasure of working with, who have given me grounding in my experiences. You know who you are.

A special acknowledgment to Bruce Pringle, who recently retired as the Director of Staff Human Resources at the University of Michigan, and who was my mentor for most of my career. He made a big difference in my life.

Table of Contents

Foreword

Every time you pick up a book, you no doubt consider whether reading it is worth your time and effort. *Management Experience Acquired* is about the leadership and skills required to be a successful manager. These skills are learned and acquired through experience and practice. This book, through text and examples, will show you what it takes to be a great manager.

Are leaders born? In family-owned businesses they are. So if you are a Gates, Ford, Hilton, or similarly situated, good for you—you probably do not need to read any further. However, managerial expertise and excellence are not found in DNA. The characteristics of successful and respected managers are acquired. Successful managers have many similar characteristics in common, and managerial skills are transferable between employers. As you read *Management Experience Acquired*, consider the examples and lessons that you can learn from our constant companion and guide—Joe.

Consider two very real errors that you have probably observed, the first made by an employer and the second by an inexperienced or insecure manager. First, a common fault in business is to promote the most productive and/or popular employees to positions of leadership over the area where they worked. The best nurse or teacher is probably not the best head nurse or school principal, yet such decisions are made by many organizations, and the results can be disastrous. Second, many newly promoted managers believe that the key to success in their job is to be popular and liked by their employees. Remember back to your school days, and consider the teacher that you now respect the most. That teacher was probably not the most popular, lenient, or easiest grader, but rather the one who had high standards and expectations, was consistent, and was available to help you when you had a problem.

There are numerous books on management. Being a good manager is not easy, and despite some books' claims, it takes a bit more than a minute. I sincerely believe this book is important to anyone who supervises, or aspires to a managerial job.

I have known author Wendy Powell for many years. She is a recognized leader in all aspects of management and human resources. She knows her subject and writes in an enjoyable, easy to read, and humorous manner. She has worked with, and is respected by, students of management and all employees—from the president to the maintenance worker. Wendy is appreciated as an internal resource and consultant for the organizations where she has worked. This book contains actual workplace examples that are common to all employers. I know you will enjoy this book. If you are serious about managing people, this book is well worth your time. Enjoy.

Bruce Pringle
Retired Director of Staff Human Resources
at the University of Michigan

Introduction

We're all looking for simple, right? And as a manager, you realize the power you have over your employees. It's daunting to think about your control over the livelihood, future, and general state of well-being of your staff. This is balanced by your responsibilities to your organization.

This is a critical responsibility that you must assume with a high degree of consciousness regardless of your level of management. Managers regularly ask about how to manage with responsibility to their organizations, as well as with fairness to their employees.

Your organization wants you to be results driven—to get the most out of your employees.

You want your resources to be close so you can quickly and painlessly get over the anguish of correcting a problem with an employee. The reality is that it's not always possible to rely on others to assist you to manage your staff. Can you afford expensive consultants and staff to handle employee problems? Most likely not. These difficult financial times often limit resources for assistance in handling management problems. Further, your boss expects you to remedy workplace issues. That's what you get paid the big bucks for, right? After all, you are the boss—or do your employees manage you?

So you are a new manager? Or a seasoned expert who wants to validate your management style? Are you studying to reach that goal? Want some refreshing information that will provide some ease and confidence to your style? Have you moved to a new organization that has new expectations? Are you a boss who has been trained and is ready to take on any workplace issue? Not many of us are. Do you have knowledge of all types of workplace issues? It's doubtful. Are you a student of management who wants to manage people with dignity and responsibility to your employer? If so, this book is the resource you need to help you achieve your goals.

I have worked on management issues for over twenty-five years and have not yet handled every type of employee problem. For most problems, though, I have been able to learn along the way, utilizing the experience I've gained from specific cases to determine a solid course of action. You'll see this as you read through this book.

In your management toolkit, you will want to have common remedies and case examples that will ease your management pain. You most definitely want to know how to hire the right employee the right way; "on-board" and "out-board" employees properly; provide corrective discipline; commend employees; respond to employee complaints; and, eminently important, protect yourself from claims and grievances. You want practical, experience-based advice at your fingertips so you can concentrate on the business issues at hand.

Management Experience Acquired will provide the advice and information you need, and will perhaps validate the good manager that you have already become. This book provides a design for supervision that will yield great results and turn you into a well-respected and grounded manager.

Do you want to become a good successful manager? Do you want assurance that you are the manager you want to be?

What *Management Experience Acquired* is *not*, is a rule book or cookbook containing pop management initiatives. You *will not* find a black belt or Malcolm Baldrige template, but you will find common sense and thought-provoking recommendations. This is a book about managing people. In difficult times, you will be called upon to handle a myriad of issues and problems. Will you be prepared?

The information I provide in this book is practical. I hope you will think, *I knew that.* This will validate the solid common sense that a good leader must have. The information in *Management Experience Acquired* is based on the questions that managers have most frequently asked me in my years of management consulting. As a human resources consultant, director of human resources, and college professor of human capital management, I have worked with thousands of leaders and aspiring managers who want practical experience they can rely on. I can't tell you how many times new managers have said to me, "I just got promoted—now what?" We automatically assume that if employees are good technicians, good secretaries, good administrative assistants, or good custodians, they will make good supervisors. Think again.

Employees may have the knowledge and ability to do a job, but do they have leadership capabilities? And can leadership ability be taught, or is it an inherent skill? Sure, there are natural leaders, but we all can grow and learn to be excellent managers.

Who is Joe? He is an employee who takes on many forms: Joe the manager, Joe the office assistant, Joe the custodian, Joe the plumber, Joe the director. He is your employee, who needs your help to become a good employee and make *you* look good. It's pretty simple. To be a good manager, you need to understand management rights and responsibilities, create good standards for your workplace, know how to correct problems and discipline employees, and know how to measure the success of your staff. Remember, practice makes perfect. *Management Experience Acquired* gives you practical management experience.

What works? Don't expect to know it all out of the starting gate. Information that you learn along the way will ground your style and practice. Over time, you will realize what is reasonable and logical in your workplace. You will reach that point with practice, but make it good practice—practice that is consistent with the mission of your organization. Cut your management teeth on good, logical experiences.

The information in this book is tried and true in every sense. I have used these principles and management philosophies for over twenty-five years to educate master's and baccalaureate students and thousands of new and seasoned managers, as well as clients through outside consulting. My students encouraged me to create *Management Experience Acquired*, and were proud to be the catalyst behind me.

Included are my versions of "Grim Tales of Management Problems." While identifying information has been changed, all of these cases have a basis in real experiences. Of course, any resemblance to actual persons is coincidental.

Managers want and need learning experiences taken from case studies—the most common requests for consultation. "What has the other guy done with these circumstances?"

My career has spanned both public and private sectors, education, county government, banking, and even a culinary school. I have learned that techniques to manage people are universal, with differences arising primarily out of management philosophy. You will see on these pages that there is a simple technique to managing people. If you follow and practice this wise management technique, you *will* be a solid, well-respected manager with a good reputation for leadership.

First, remember to take your time reading this book. Don't read it all in one sitting. There is a logical progression to the material and cases that will build upon each of the learning experiences. Refer to www.managementexperienceacquired.com for actual sample letters, settlement agreements, performance evaluations, and more. Some samples are included in the appendixes of this book as well.

At the end of each section, you will find Relevant Questions to Consider. You can apply the principles found in these sections to your workplace, your experiences, or your future aspirations. Please take the time to think about each question and how it relates to you and your employer.

Joe the Employee

Joe entered the office; it was late and the downtown lights were already twinkling—but ominously. He entered without announcing his presence, but his presence was not a surprise. He tugged on his tie and fell into the chair in desperate wonderment. "The boss thinks I am the most ridiculous, uninformed person she's ever met," he announced. "I guess there is nothing else for me to do but quit."

Quit? Now Joe had worked diligently on his latest project, adding his own style of confidence and polish to the finished product. But he was a failure in his boss's eyes, receiving public ridicule from her for what she perceived as his inept performance. Joe muttered, "If only they would've told me the new direction they were taking and the details they expected. Are they spoon-feeding me information and not giving me the whole picture? Was this a setup? They must want me to leave. Go figure." In all actuality, Joe's project was a great piece of work, but it was not recognized for its quality. The reality was that he was at the mercy of his boss.

Mind you, Joe is an employee with a sterling reputation in his field. He has succeeded for more than twenty years in business without a single blemish on his record. Joe relocated to this new company and suddenly, he couldn't tie his shoes without being ridiculed and micromanaged. He moved on to another job. Unlucky manager! She lost a great employee.

Joe is your employee, your colleague, or even you.

When you have a problem employee, think about the time you invested in the recruiting and training process. Think about the employee downtime you experienced while you waited for the long employment process to be over. Think about the fact that there was something that sparked your interest in this employee who is now failing to please you as a manager. Your first thought should be, *Can I save this employee?* Your second thought should be, *Do I want to save the employee, and what hoops do I have to jump through to do it?* Is there an agenda to terminate?

As the manager of an inadequate employee, you *always* need to think, *Why is this problem occurring?* and *What do I need to do next?* You need a blueprint to go into action. Think about the fact that you need to be prepared to deal with problems before they occur.

Help your employees to be successful. It's a pretty simple concept, with many issues in tow. Think about the best boss you've ever had and the worst boss you've ever had. Chances are the best boss provided clear instruction, good feedback, and allowed you the freedom to do your job well. The worst boss likely provided no vision or direction, and berated your every move. We've all heard the adage, "You catch more flies with honey than vinegar." Remember it.

Relevant Questions to Consider

Let's begin. Ask yourself, *Do I make the goal of employee success my priority as a manager?* How so? List the ways you review and examine employee success. If you are comfortable with your list, great. Is your list in keeping with the boss's agenda and the company's strategy? If you need to work on your list, think about initiatives that would improve the success of your employees. If you are a new manager or a student of management, begin planning your course of action.

____

____

____

____

Chapter 1

What is Your "Brand"?

Joe the Upwardly Mobile

Joe has an irritating work style. His work is okay, and he gets by because he can do an effective job, but he has a reputation of being controlling and uncooperative.

You have an opening in your department, and Joe applies. You know his shortcomings, but you need someone who is experienced and can step into the job immediately. You know Joe can. Besides that, your boss knows Joe and she supports his candidacy, and of course, you want to please your boss. You are confident in your skills as a manager, and so Joe is hired into your department.

Joe immediately starts meeting with your boss behind your back on a regular basis. Yikes! You realize that this is a takeover. You knew his "brand" before you hired him. You fell into this trap. This was a disguised attempt at a "palace coup." He wanted to take over your department. You need to confront this head-on.

Unfortunately, this type of behavior is quite common. Be confident in your abilities, but make sure that Joe understands the appropriate protocols about working with senior management.

Joe had the reputation, or brand, that preceded him.

Look at the brand of employee you want to hire. I don't think you are searching for an uncooperative, irritating, controlling maverick who wants to take over your job. What is *your* brand? Take a good look at yourself. What reputation do you want as a leader? Ask yourself, *Who do I emulate and what qualities does he or she have?*

When the time comes for the next step in your career, you want to possess a solid character that screams, "I am the one for this job!" You want your name to say reliable, accountable, accomplished, responsive, and pleasant. Or, depending on the boss, your name could say merciless, cunning, and shrewd. You want to back up these qualities by demonstrating examples of your branding. Of course, you want to be known as the best at what you do, but be clear about the direction that suits you.

Managers that lack finesse end up losing in the end, at least most of the time. Don't hedge your bets with this; bad form will bite you, whether it means lost productivity, turnover costs, or loss of your credibility as a manager. Believe me, I've seen it in action many times, and it's not pretty. Treat employees with respect; emulate the behavior that you expect from them. It's simple but true: you choose your brand, and it stays with you.

Relevant Questions to Consider

Ask yourself, *What is my brand?* and *What do I want on my "management epitaph"?* Be critical and honest with your evaluation of yourself. List the qualities that come to mind. This list will help you conduct your own personal critical appraisal, and identify issues you can work on to further your progress toward great management.

____

____

____

____

____

Good Boss, Bad Boss, Cookbook Boss

I'm guessing that your worst boss did not prepare you for your job, left you wondering if you were performing the job well, and was likely quick to criticize your work—basically treating you like you should rethink your career choice. Does that sound familiar? There is a school of thought that says to make it to the top of management, you need to be tough and always look to rid yourself of the bottom 10 percent of your workforce; this will take care of performance problems. *Don't be that guy or gal.* Be careful with this. Your star employees who suddenly start performing poorly may just be having a rough time, and could likely rebound with coaching and grooming. If you were to fire one, you could lose a jewel who could ultimately make you look good as a manager.

Let's rethink this issue. Which way do you want to manage? Your job is to help employees succeed in your workplace. At some point in your career, though, you will need to discipline and fire employees. In fact, this will happen with some regularity. But when you do have to make that move, make sure it is done on a case-by-case basis, taking into account the particular facts of the employee—the whole picture.

Shouldn't we treat everyone exactly the same?

No. The answer to this question has regularly surprised students of management and supervisors alike.

Instead of equal treatment, think equitable treatment.

What the heck is that? We all understand equal treatment. Isn't it an expected, God-given right? A common phrase used by one exceptionally bad manager I knew was, "Treat 'em good, treat 'em bad, treat 'em all the same." She thought that philosophy would protect her in case of a challenge. This particularly bad boss was eventually fired.

Treating everyone equally badly does not protect a boss from claims and grievances. In fact, it encourages employees to talk around the water cooler, compare notes, and potentially file a class action suit. On the other hand, equitable treatment means fair and reasonable consideration of all of the facts concerning an employee problem.

Joe the Terminally Ill Employee

Let's look at this issue: Joe has a clean record, a great work ethic, and has worked with you for five years. Sue has worked with you for one year, and you've counseled her for tardiness and unsatisfactory work performance. Are you going to handle a problem with Joe's performance exactly the same as you would a problem with Sue's? I sure hope not. You need to consider the whole employee, not just the specific problem.

Some organizations take a "cookbook" approach to managing people. A cookbook is a management tool or policy that does not take into consideration the specifics of the individual employee. For example, an attendance policy that states that if an employee is absent on five occasions in a three-month period, he will be disciplined. Of course, employees can understand this standard. It's simple. But does it yield the results that you want? Probably not in all cases.

Case in point: Joe was legitimately absent due to his fight with cancer. He had used up all of his time under the Family and Medical Leave Act and had missed enough work that he was up for termination the next time he was sick.

Joe went into the hospital one final time. He and his family were in serious danger of losing their benefits, life insurance, and income if he lost his job. Joe's family asked for time to apply for long-term disability—a leave without pay to permit them to get their affairs in order. Unfortunately, the organization had no such policy for long-term benefits. Joe was called at the hospital and terminated. He died the next week. Despite Joe's twenty years of service to the organization, no exception was made for his absence due to terminal illness. Unfortunate situations like this can occur when all employees are treated equally, rather than equitably.

The moral of this story is that as a manager, you should use common sense and create new policies when needs arise, make exceptions when necessary, and learn from the experience. Of course, you need to get the support of HR or organizational leadership to make significant changes to policy.

Think about how you would like to be treated if you were in the hot seat.

Go beyond the surface, look at the details, ask yourself, *Why is this policy in place? Does it need to be revised for this situation, based on the facts?* Remember, you are in direct control of Joe's livelihood. A move you make must be grounded and sensible. For Heaven's sake, consider all of the facts and document your reasons for exceptions. Remember, there was something you liked about Joe when you hired him, so take special circumstances into account.

This logic goes a long way. Managers don't show weakness by treating employees with respect, even when there is a need for performance correction. When you are considering whether to discipline or discharge Joe, you need to examine all of the facts and ask yourself why Joe is having problems.

- Why is this occurring?
- Why do I want or need to fire Joe?
- Why make an exception for Joe?
- What would be the impact on my organization if I make an exception for Joe?

Prior to any involuntary termination, I strongly recommend that you hold a disciplinary review meeting with the employee to discuss the reasons that you are considering a separation. This provides due process for employees and gives you an opportunity to hear their side of the story. You may discover that you need to do more investigation into the problem. This is particularly valuable when there is an appeal of the termination. Get your facts straight and complete. This entire process helps put work issues into perspective.

A few things to consider when deciding how to resolve a problem with an employee:

- Look at Joe's entire personnel history. Has he been disciplined? If so, is it related to the current problem? Has he been employed for ten years with no problems? Or six months with reoccurring issues?

- What's going on with Joe? Are there problems in his outside world that are causing the issues he's having at work? Does he need the assistance of a professional to help him to correct the problem, perhaps by a referral to an employee assistance program?
- Do you have any policies that dictate how you should handle his problem? How have you treated this type of problem in the past? Is there a clear precedence?

Relevant Questions to Consider

Ask yourself, *Do I consider all of the facts when up against a problem employee?* Or is it simpler to treat everyone exactly the same? Do you use a cookbook approach? Have you ever made a decision that you regret concerning your staff? Have you seen a colleague make a bad employment decision? How could additional critical thinking have affected the outcome of those cases?

____

____

____

____

____

Chapter 2

First of All, Hire 'em Right!

I can't tell you how often I have heard managers say, "I should have spent more time in the interview process; I didn't hire the right person. If only I had not been in such a hurry to fill that spot." In a flurry of unfinished work, managers often make hasty hiring decisions, ultimately forcing them to spend countless hours fixing their hiring mistakes. We have all done it.

When you have a job opening, it gives you an opportunity to look at the job description to see if you have described the position well. Take a critical look at the *duties* as well as the *qualifications.* Have you employed staff who expected an employment experience that was not clearly outlined from the beginning? Be clear about the duties of the job; don't leave the job open to interpretation. If the description is vague, it is likely you'll have to start the laborious search process all over again, when the newly hired employee doesn't work out.

A typical error is illustrated by a want ad seeking an administrative assistant to perform high-level administrative support to an executive, when, in reality, the company is looking for a personal assistant to maintain the boss's calendar and type letters. The person the company hires will not remain in the position if the expectations and duties are incorrectly described.

The same applies to qualifications. Be realistic. The office assistant to the chemistry department chair does not need a master's degree in chemistry to perform basic administrative support. Again, don't make this mistake; describe the whole picture well so the employee will not be surprised with the work. Unwanted turnover will take you away from your own work—and your bottom line.

Think carefully about the selection criteria and other qualifications for the job. Develop qualifications that you will use to measure candidates for your job. Careful examination and creation of specific criteria will help protect you from any claims against your selection, as you will be able to quickly point to the reasons you selected the candidate who most closely matched your criteria.

When creating your selection criteria, take a look at job postings on online recruiting sites such as Monster.com or CareerBuilder.com. You'll notice that job qualifications are generally well-defined.

For example, the following job posting for a payroll employee on the web site CareerBuilder.com outlined the company's selection criteria. The expectations are clearly stated, as is the background that is essential for success on the job.

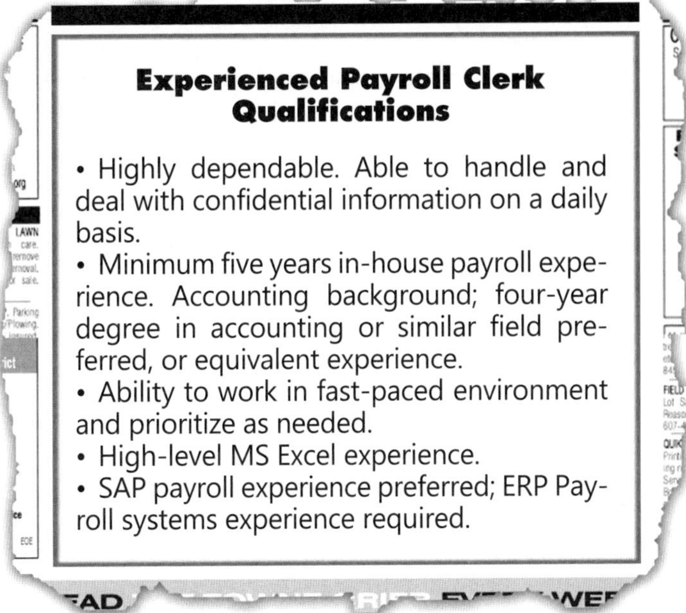

Experienced Payroll Clerk
Qualifications

- Highly dependable. Able to handle and deal with confidential information on a daily basis.
- Minimum five years in-house payroll experience. Accounting background; four-year degree in accounting or similar field preferred, or equivalent experience.
- Ability to work in fast-paced environment and prioritize as needed.
- High-level MS Excel experience.
- SAP payroll experience preferred; ERP Payroll systems experience required.

Advertise your available position in an exciting way, such as this excellent posting from Monster.com, written by Recruiting Goddess Bridget O'Connor. Bridget is a colleague of mine and former president of BKO Enterprises, a well-respected recruiting firm with a long track record of success.

This type of advertisement will leave the candidates with a positive feeling about working for you and your organization. These candidates raved about the posting. Who wouldn't want to work here?

Writer/Editor—PHENOMENAL entry-level opportunity—great bennies including 30 days PTO!

We are currently looking for an exceptional entry-level writer to join our communications team led by our incredibly impressive and humorous chief communications officer (she gave me chocolate to say that). Her team is made up of talented, friendly, and helpful individuals who always have smiles on their faces (*they* haven't given me any chocolate yet, but they will).

Here's the thing. We have so many exciting events and activities going on in our organization every day that the communications department is constantly under the gun to get the information out to their audiences. The organization has therefore created a new entry-level writing position to spread some of the fun to. This is an incredible opportunity for someone just starting out their writing career after completing their bachelor's degree. This diverse writing position will be involved in a wide range of exciting activities including but not limited to:

• (Bulleted job description appeared here.)

Requirements:

• (Bulleted requirements appeared here.)

So, you think you're the one for the job? Then prove it! Apply online with your résumé, along with an impromptu creative writing sample. The subject, you ask? Why we should hire you! This is your chance to demonstrate your writing skills, creativity, and perhaps your proficiency

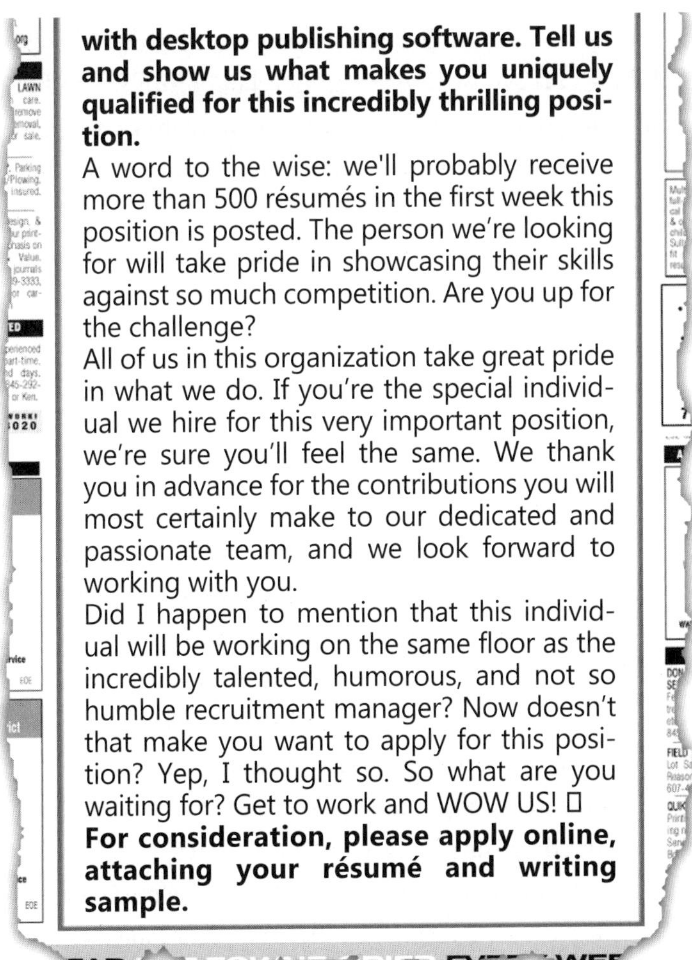

with desktop publishing software. Tell us and show us what makes you uniquely qualified for this incredibly thrilling position.

A word to the wise: we'll probably receive more than 500 résumés in the first week this position is posted. The person we're looking for will take pride in showcasing their skills against so much competition. Are you up for the challenge?

All of us in this organization take great pride in what we do. If you're the special individual we hire for this very important position, we're sure you'll feel the same. We thank you in advance for the contributions you will most certainly make to our dedicated and passionate team, and we look forward to working with you.

Did I happen to mention that this individual will be working on the same floor as the incredibly talented, humorous, and not so humble recruitment manager? Now doesn't that make you want to apply for this position? Yep, I thought so. So what are you waiting for? Get to work and WOW US! ☐

For consideration, please apply online, attaching your résumé and writing sample.

This incredible job advertisement sets the stage for the personality of the company. Remember, you want to grab the attention of candidates so they will want to work for you and not your competitor. Be sure to highlight the focus of the job in the headline, such as this ad did with, "Writer/ Editor—PHENOMENAL entry-level opportunity," and of course, let your personality shine through. Don't be afraid to be lighthearted. Employees want to enjoy their workplace, so demonstrate your strengths.

Some great tips for writing a job advertisement include:

- Be specific on the job responsibilities and use action words.
- Make sure you are clear about the qualifications. Realize that you may need to sift through hundreds of résumés, so do yourself a favor and stop unqualified candidates from applying in the first place by describing the ideal candidate in detail.
- If you have great benefits, say so. A free gym membership or a chef on the premises could be extremely enticing perks to a prospective employee.
- Don't worry about the size of your ad. Work within your advertising budget and consider where you will get the most bang for your buck with the more difficult recruiting challenges. This sample is long, but it will yield exactly the type of employee they are looking for.
- Remember, it's an employment jungle out there. There are hundreds of candidates for each job, so it is easy for the great candidates to get lost in the application process. Look carefully at the candidates

who make their qualifications stand out. In fact, seek out the résumés that list accomplishments. It shows a good track record of success.

After you have decided on your list of qualified candidates, create interview questions directly related to the job that will highlight the candidate's experience. You want to know about their critical thinking skills. Use the same questions for all the candidates that will be interviewed. The value of using the same questions is in the results—you will be able to consistently judge the quality of the responses, and you will be protected from accusations of differential treatment in the hiring process. Use phrases that give you insight into their workplace behavior such as:

- How did you handle…?
- What was your biggest challenge with an employee-related matter?
- What are your thoughts about…?

These types of questions will reveal the candidates' critical thinking abilities in direct relation to the responsibilities of the job.

Provide each member of your interviewing team with a template of the questions and have them rate each candidate. Keep the information that has been completed by the interviewing team for at least three years, in case there is any challenge to your hiring decision. Also, caution the team about recording their comments appropriately. Most of us know the consequences of inappropriate selection comments. On one occasion, I was working with a manager who was interviewing candidates. On his interview notes, he wrote the editorial comment, "Nice legs." Enough said.

Remember, hire the right person with the right qualifications for the job. Don't get stuck with a new employee who can't perform the basics.

If you need to hire someone immediately, there are many reputable temp agencies that can provide you with a credible replacement to handle basic work. Check them out—you may even find a good candidate for your vacancy.

Joe the Supervisor in Waiting

Joe was encouraged. The position in his company he had been waiting for was finally posted. He had more than ten years of experience in all aspects of the selection criteria for the job in question. He spoke with HR, and they assured him that he was a great match for the job. He was a shoo-in—or so he thought.

Joe interviewed well, describing his vast experience with widgets in great detail, a desired qualification mentioned in the job description. *Hmm*, he thought. *This is going well. I'm finally going to land my dream job.* There was silence in the following week from HR. Joe took it to mean that they had to consider other candidates as a formality—he wasn't worried.

On Monday morning, the memo arrived. "Patricia has decided to pursue other candidates at this time whose qualifications and experience more closely match what the position requires," it read. Joe was left wondering, *What happened to my job? Am I overqualified? Do they want a "fresh out of college" candidate?*

Well, the answer was "yes." Joe was the most qualified candidate, but someone else was better "suited" for the job.

Be very careful of this scenario. Thoughts can race about age or sex discrimination, preferential treatment, or nepotism if the hiring decision is suspect. You want the person who will be able to best perform the specific job, right?

If you want new blood, explain what experience you want. If you want an intern, say so. Don't harbor unrealistic expectations of your candidates. You may invite claims and lawsuits.

Employment situations such as this are rather transparent. Don't use the explanation of someone being "overqualified." Technically, there is no such animal. Your candidate may have infinite qualifications, but you may choose to ratchet down the responsibilities and selection criteria for the job, and hire someone else. Remember, be clear about your expectations. You don't want to have to defend your hiring decision with an internal superstar candidate waiting in the wings.

Joe watched the newly hired former intern struggle with her lack of experience in his dream position. Joe visited a lawyer, but took no legal action. Lucky, lucky boss! He decided that he didn't want to work for someone who did not choose him for the job, so he quit. Joe realized that he could not reach his career goals in this organization. It was a loss to the organization, as well as Joe.

Joe the Inexperienced HR Manager

Joe is the team leader of the data processing crew. Your HR manager suddenly resigned and you cannot leave the position vacant. Joe is a great employee. Everyone respects him. Anybody can do HR, right? So you promote Joe to the position. Reluctantly, Joe takes the job, despite the fact that he knows nothing about managing an HR function.

It is quickly discovered that he has no knowledge of recruiting, compensation, or employee relations. Managers go to him for assistance and soon learn that Joe is incompetent. *Incompetent?* He is a smart guy. He has been promoted to his level of incompetence. Joe had the ability to learn, but you needed someone to get the job done in quick order. Demoralized, Joe left. He was replaced. You lost a great employee.

Beware of the "Peter Principle." You may not know what the principle is, but I'm sure you have seen it in action. It is simply a rule developed by Dr. Laurence Peter and Raymond Hull in 1968. The principle asserts that employees generally reach their level of competency and then tend to get promoted to positions in which they have no competency.

Though satirical in presentation, it was quickly realized that Peter and Hull's message was grounded in management reality. It is generally assumed that if an employee does his job well, he will also do well in the next level up the corporate ladder. Have you seen it in action? Sure. Often, a career-crushing blow can happen to the employee because of his inability to perform in a new, higher-level position. But the question is: should he ever have been put in that position in the first place?

Relevant Questions to Consider

Do you have a process in place to review the job duties, qualifications, and interview questions for your candidates? Think about an example of when you may have made a hasty hiring decision and hired the wrong person for the job. Think about the long-term effects of maintaining the wrong employee and the trouble it caused, and the time and excessive effort it wasted. What would you do differently next time?

____

____

____

____

____

Chapter 3

On-boarding: A Good Start

Joe the New Widget Processor

When Joe was hired into his widget-processing position, his manager assigned a peer mentor to help him through his first days on the job. This mentor worked with Joe to show him the ropes. His mentor was instructed to introduce Joe to his coworkers in a positive manner so he could establish relationships without preconceived notions. He explained expense reports, phone usage, where to go to lunch, and where to pick up his paycheck, along with other general tips, helping to create a semblance of normalcy for Joe. This increased his comfort level in the new and unfamiliar environment. Joe's boss also gave his mentor a small budget to organize a welcoming activity for Joe. Assigning the responsibility to a specific mentor gives Joe a direct point of contact for questions or concerns.

I remember my first day on the job at Acme University, working as an employee relations representative. I was welcomed with the usual handshake and escorted to my office where policy manuals, unfamiliar binders, and various documents awaited my arrival. There was nothing more, no orientation to the job. My boss expected me to "hit the ground running." After all, I was hired to bring my experience to the job and start working with no training.

Oh no! How can someone thrive in a job with no orientation, acclimation, or training? What's the workplace culture? What are the expectations? It happens all of the time—new employees are expected to jump up and perform with little or no standards or expectations.

Do you remember *your* first day on the job? Let's face it, there's no way around it; it's tough. It ranks up there with life's most stressful experiences. The next time you see a group of new employees on the job, stop and observe. Introduce yourself to them with a warm handshake. You would have appreciated the same welcome.

I recently had the experience of visiting the workplace of a friend who is an office manager in a doctor's office. When I walked into the office, I saw a wall filled with manuals, binders, and patient records. It reminded me of my previous experience of starting a new job without training or specific instructions about the workplace culture. I felt that same old feeling about what it's like for a new employee starting work with no grooming and orientation.

I couldn't step into my role at Acme University without knowing the ropes. While I knew how to perform my job responsibilities and I had the experience and qualifications, I did not know the ins and outs of the organization. My boss expected me to know it all without any instruction. Without careful acclimation, the results can be disastrous. You may lose your best employees without a smart start. This is where on-boarding comes into play.

It's helpful for managers to create an orientation checklist to provide new employees with clear direction and expected standards, including organizational policies and departmental norms. This document identifies the issues that will be discussed with new employees, such as particular job expectations, job description, working hours, and the consequences for lack of adherence to policies.

Socialize your new employee in your workplace environment to give him or her a positive start. This simple template works:

The first day (or before):

- Schedule the new employee to meet with HR to discuss requisite paperwork: I-9s, tax forms, benefits forms, etc.
- Present the new employee with the offer letter and address any questions concerning the employment relationship. Be clear about conditions of employment and review the job description and expectations.

- Set up new employee's desk and computer for immediate use on the first day. This provides a little bit of personal ownership in the new workplace.
- Provide a simple but welcoming surprise: have a small plant, box of candy, or bouquet of flowers with well wishes from coworkers on the new employee's desk or work area.
- Schedule a meeting with a member of the information technology (IT) department to explain login information and how to access critical programs.
- Make sure basic office supplies, such as pens, paper, stapler, and other essentials, are ready at the work location. It seems like common sense, but it doesn't always happen. Order business cards (if applicable).
- Provide a current employee directory. Explain the key players in your organization—you don't want the new employee to not recognize the president.

In the first week:

- Meet with the new employee to discuss orientation issues, including benefits and pertinent policies for review. Send an electronic version of topics discussed in the meeting and other essential information to the new employee for review. If there are several new employees hired within a short time frame, the meeting can be held with the entire group.

- Introduce the new employee to key colleagues and take him on a tour of the building.
- Provide the new employee with the vision and mission statement of your organization. Tell him how his responsibilities fit into that vision and discuss policies pertinent to his new department.

After three weeks:

- Discuss the progress of the new employee's orientation and ask if there are questions and/or issues that need clarification. A further review of the employee's personal data should be done to make sure that the information in the system is accurate and the employee has enrolled in benefits (if applicable).
- Invite the new employee to team meetings so he can become familiar with the work of colleagues.
- Invite the new employee to a senior management meeting in the first weeks of hire to introduce him- or herself and meet senior leadership staff.
- Don't leave the new employee "hanging out to dry." Invite him or her to lunch or have a coworker do so.
- Assign the new employee a mentor. The mentor is a valued and trusted colleague in the employee's department who can share information particular to the department. (Create a checklist of material for the mentor to use in discussion with the new employee.)

- Have the mentor assist the new employee on a daily basis for at least one month and then check in weekly, monthly, etc., as necessary.
- Permit the new employee to "shadow" the mentor as often as is practical in the first week(s).

A month later:

- Check in with the new employee to evaluate the status of his or her progress and address any questions related to his or her department.
- Update your boss and your human resources department with the new employee's progress. See if there have been any snags with his or her start at the organization that need to be sorted out, and see if any additional grooming is necessary.

Relevant Questions to Consider

Ask yourself, *Have I started my employees off right?* If so, reaffirm your success. If not, ask yourself, *What would I do differently to assist new employees with their on-boarding?* Create a list and check it twice. Identify the things that Joe would need to be successful in your workplace.

____

____

____

____

Chapter 4

Setting Standards

Joe the Restroom Supervisor

Joe contacted me with a concern about his staff taking too many trips to the restroom. Joe claimed that he intended to create a new standard that allowed his staff to only use the restroom a maximum of ten minutes per hour. On the surface, that may not be an overly restrictive standard. But, when I asked him how he intended to monitor and control the standard, he indicated that he would spend time in the hallway by the restroom to assure compliance. When I asked him if that was how he planned on spending his time, being a restroom monitor, he realized the standard was neither reasonable nor controllable.

Had Joe met with the staff to discuss his concern and created a collective remedy to the situation, this problem could have been avoided.

Focus on the work product and the expected standards; it will lead you in the right direction to solve problems. Don't waste your time with tasks that will take you away from your real management responsibilities.

Are your expectations and rules reasonable, believable, and controllable? Employees need to know where they stand.

One of the most important responsibilities of supervisors is to set standards for their staff. While not all standards need to be put in writing, most of the nuances of a particular workplace should be made known to the employees. Office standards can encompass many issues, such as working hours, break times, dress and appearance, and phone and computer usage.

First and foremost, make sure employees understand the standard that you are creating. In fact, involve them in its creation. Schedule team meetings to discuss changes that are coming down the pike, and solicit participation from the employees. Explain the rationale for the standard and why it is necessary, and ask for input and buy-in. You will be amazed at their willingness to participate.

Secondly, when a standard is established, it should be reviewed under the proverbial microscope to determine if it is reasonable and controllable. If a standard is viewed as overly restrictive or intolerable, it will be difficult to garner support for it from your employees and even more difficult to enforce.

Finally, when you change an existing standard, the same applies; create a team of reliable employees to assist in the transition and provide methods for accomplishing the new goal. The employees are the ones to carry out the standard, so involve them. Don't always assume that employees understand the new standard. Take time to explain the change and provide the background and rationale for the reasons behind the change. It will pay off.

A general rule of thumb applies here:

Departments cannot create standards that violate the overriding policies of the organization or the mission and vision statements.

Managers should not independently go out on a limb to create their own operating policies that are not in keeping with the philosophies of the organization. Deviations that override operating policies need to be carefully evaluated and approved by senior management. Don't put yourself out there without thorough review and support.

For example, if an organization has a policy that employees cannot drink alcohol on their lunch breaks and a manager creates a departmental standard that a cocktail with a client at lunch is permissible, that manager will face repercussions from the higher-ups for overriding a standard policy without clearing it first.

Relevant Questions to Consider

Grade yourself on how well your employees understand and are able to meet your workplace standards. List your own standards in your workplace, examine them, scrutinize them, and audit your rules, as well as employee compliance and acceptance of them. Ask yourself, *What are the critical needs for clarification in my real or virtual department? What do I need to do to create standards to clarify my expectations?*

____

____

____

____

____

Chapter 5

Change and More Change

Joe the Uninformed Change Agent

Wanting to make a name for himself in the organization, Joe, the new manager, announced to the well-seasoned staff, "We need to change." What? Just change for the sake of change? There was no discussion of problems or environmental needs for change, just change itself.

Soon after, there was a flurry of sidebar meetings to gossip about why there was a need to change. The confused employees said among themselves, "After all, to our customers, we are well-respected and trusted employees. We know the business better than Joe!"

Joe attempted to start fresh with his new staff, hoping to make a difference and a name for himself. He thought, *They will love the changes that I make. Let's mix them up and give them new client groups.* He scrambled their responsibilities, putting them in unfamiliar territory. Joe was met with confusion and frustration from his staff. He thought, *It's out with the old and in with the new, and it's time they learn new responsibilities.* He made a difference all right: the customers were upset because they had a comfort level with their client reps and valued the contributions and knowledge of the staff.

Joe lost the trust of the customers, who complained, "What is Joe doing? He doesn't understand our needs."

Afraid of change? I am. We all are, to some degree. Change begins with the unknown and brings challenges along the way. Organizational leaders are wed to it and expect it. Leaders are often judged by what has changed since they took office. I can't tell you how many times I've heard first-line managers say, "We have to change, and I don't know why."

If you need to manage a change initiative, you need to know what is not working and why you have to change.

The most essential part of a change initiative is that employees understand what needs to change and why.

The first rumor of impending change strikes terror in employees who may be affected by a new environment. "Will my job be eliminated or changed?" "Will I have a new boss?" "Will I have to learn new ways to do my job?" "Will I have any say-so?" "Will I be told why?"

When you are in the middle of a change initiative, ask yourself on a weekly basis, *Are the employees on board with the status of the impending changes, and have I communicated with them to make sure they are aware of the most up-to-date information?* If you lose track of these questions, you may lose the momentum necessary to smoothly transition into the new work environment. Fix any communication problems immediately; hold quick status meetings with a question and answer session. Permit employees to submit questions anonymously in advance of meetings. This prevents employees from being afraid to ask those "stupid" questions.

Even if there are only minor changes that affect your work group, the same thing applies. But in this case, you are fortunate because you have more control over the outcome since it only affects your area of control. Yes, you can make a name for yourself with change, good or bad.

Relevant Questions to Consider

Think about change initiatives that have gone awry (and we all know some). It's likely that the self-probing status questions I suggested above were not asked. How would you have changed the process? How will you handle a change initiative differently in the future?

____

____

____

____

____

Chapter 6

What Are Your Rights and Responsibilities?

"You can't tell me not to say that at work. I have my opinion, and I have the right to free speech. It says so in the Constitution!" I can't tell you how many times employees have said that to me. The fact of the matter is *no*, you can't say anything you want to in the workplace. At least not without the possibility of consequences.

Joe the Santa Claus

In the movie *Miracle on 34th Street,* Kris Kringle sent parents to other stores to buy cheaper Christmas toys for their kids. While it was a great marketing ploy at the time, the reality is a problem for sales clerks. Joe is a student who landed a job as a cashier in the college bookstore. One of his responsibilities is to sell athletic shoes. One of his friends went into the bookstore to buy shoes. Within earshot of his boss, Joe told his friend, "Don't buy the shoes here. You can get them cheaper at the local discount store...and they have better shoes."

Well, the boss pulled him aside and said, "Who are you, Kris Kringle? We have a business to run, and you had better not send our customers away." Despite the warning, when the situation presented itself again, Joe sent away another customer. No question about it, Joe was right; the shoes were cheaper at the discount store. But he still should not send customers away. He was fired. Joe said, "What about my right to free speech?" Sure, Joe has a right to free speech, but he paid the consequences after not following his boss's instructions.

Joe the Plumber

Think back to the 2008 presidential election. Most of us remember when Joe the Plumber asked a probing question of presidential candidate Barack Obama. Joe was on his own street when the candidate came to visit. Joe was invited to ask a question and what happened next created a firestorm of controversy. As a result, the media investigated Joe's background, reporting information about Joe that was unrelated to his question. Is it always safe to ask questions?

Mostly, we are comfortable in our society asking questions, even in the workplace. Whichever side of the political fence you are on, the backlash against Joe the Plumber raises a reason to pause. We think we can safely ask a question without retribution. But we should think again. We and our jobs could be affected by it.

Have you ever attended a business meeting where you were fearful of asking a "stupid question"? There is no such thing. Or is there? Are you afraid to ask a question because the boss will assume you are uninformed? Don't be. Speak up—your colleague could ask the same question and get credit for the idea, leaving you with a missed opportunity.

A middle school teacher insults a student's father, who is serving in the military, for not supporting her favored presidential candidate. Is this free speech? Some think it is. Think again: there are consequences to expressing your opinions on the job. The teacher was disciplined for insulting a student and advocating her political position at her workplace.

Joe the Confidant

Joe's boss Ted was deficient in social graces to say the least. Ted yelled at Joe in front of his coworkers, making it clear that he didn't like him. Ted was insecure and protective of his own job, the typical insecure boss who was afraid that Joe might take his job. Do you know a Ted? Many of us do.

Joe felt comfortable confiding in a director from another department. He vented about Ted's unfair treatment, micromanagement, and lack of feedback. The director listened without reaction. Joe thanked him for the opportunity to express his frustrations. Little did he know that the director was a close confidant of Ted's, and soon informed Ted of everything Joe had said.

Joe's relationship with Ted was destroyed. Within a month, Joe was encouraged to resign. Unfortunately, he had not picked his audience well.

Think before you vent to a colleague. He or she could have another agenda.

If you are going to vent, complain, or otherwise discuss your strategies for survival in your job, make sure you know and trust the person you confide in. The best rule of thumb is to always be professional and never trust that your workplace relationships will remain the same throughout your employment with the organization.

What about the occasional dirty joke? Shop talk? I can't stress enough that you need to know your audience with iron-clad confidence. Don't discuss privileged information in your workplace. Don't forget that if you create or forward an e-mail that is potentially offensive, it becomes a permanent record and can be traced back to you. If you don't want to take on that risk, don't do it. I have known of many situations that have turned into serious employment problems for employees who have not chosen their audience well. Be careful.

These are hot issues that defy clear answers, but similar issues can be raised in your organization. Don't forget that all workplace discussions are on the record. There is no rewind or delete possible after you have stated your position or asked your questions. Be careful and chose your comments wisely.

You must consider the consequences of someone's free speech in the workplace. Can an employee and his boss have a productive working relationship if the boss knows the employee was publically criticizing him or her?

With all of the laws and policies that support employees, managers often say, "What rights do *I* have?" The fact is that managers have infinite rights. The exhaustive list is dependent on the mission of the organization and the responsibility of the boss to get the work done. So, your rights simply fall squarely in the area of what needs to be done to make the organization successful.

Now the reality: with every management right that you can think of, there is a responsibility to the employee. It's a balancing act. The following are common rights and responsibilities that my colleagues and I have provided as a reminder to managers.[1]

Managers have the right to:

- Determine the work to be done and the expected standards.
- Decide the qualifications and determine if employees have the ability to perform the job.

1. University of Michigan Health System, "Management Rights and Responsibilities," http://www.med.umich.edu/umhshr/supervisor/rights-responsibilities.html.

- Determine the chosen methods for employees to perform their work.
- Plan and evaluate performance.
- Establish and change work schedules and working hours.
- Determine whether, and to what extent, work shall be performed.
- Determine employees' job descriptions and determine pay.
- Assure that the required qualifications are appropriate for the job and be consistent and realistic about their expectations.
- Change or introduce new operations, methods, and processes.
- Assign, transfer, promote, demote, discipline, release, and lay off employees.

Managers have the responsibility to:

- Be responsive to individual needs.
- Involve employees in creating changes to policies and keep an open line of communication.
- Be fair and treat employees equitably.
- Follow policies, labor agreements, and laws.
- Review classification descriptions and assign work fairly.
- Let employees know where they stand and follow policies.

Relevant Questions to Consider

Do *you* know whom you can confide in and whom you can't? Whom can you strategize with? Who won't betray your confidence?

Have you ever said to your employees, "I can do this because I am the boss and I have the right to"? That's not good form. Think about the rights you have as a manager, as well as your responsibilities to your staff. List policies and laws that you need to research.

____

____

____

____

____

Don't "Delegate Up," My Friend. Have a Plan!

Think through the expected duties of a position, the problems you have with an employee's performance of those duties, and how you plan to assist the employee to correct the workplace problems.

This is what I said to Joe. He was a new supervisor when he discovered problems with the performance of his assistant. Joe wrote an impressive list of his assistant's shortcomings, went to the boss, and asked him what he should do. Joe's boss retorted, "I understand the problem, but are you telling *me* to fix it?"

This is not good form. You need to have a plan about how to fix the problem yourself.

Many managers make this mistake. They think bringing problems to the attention of their boss is the right and responsible thing to do. Well, sure, the boss needs to know, but you need to complete an important step prior to going to the boss. When you go to your boss, always propose a solution or two to the problem you present. In fact, many bosses will want more than one to consider. Ask yourself, *What are my options?* Without your suggestions to correct the problem, the boss may question your managerial skills. Show your analytical ability. Be specific with the facts, and provide your rationale.

Relevant Questions to Consider

Think about a time when you brought a problem to your boss. Did you propose a solution—or two? If so, were they grounded? Did you provide rationale, statistics? How would this change your reputation with your boss? What, if anything, would you change about *your* approach?

____

____

____

____

____

Chapter 7

Flexibility in the Workplace

Joe the Needy Coworker

Joe and Mary work in the same office. They each have their own personal needs and interests. Joe is attending night school, and Mary is a single mom with many family responsibilities. Both Joe and Mary request accommodation for their own unique needs and work schedules. What's a boss to do? How do you work out special arrangements with two valued employees when you have to get a job done?

A supervisor can meet both the required staffing needs of the department and the scheduling needs of employees by using alternative scheduling arrangements. Flexibility in the workplace has stemmed from a need for employees to balance quality of life issues with professional expectations. Employers with budgetary constraints can benefit from alternative scheduling as well. The challenge for leadership is to balance these needs with the critical staffing requirements of a department.

One solution is to agree upon flexible working hours, which results in a schedule outside of the typical nine to five, and which meets the needs of both the employer and employee. According to the Department of Labor, in 2004, approximately 27.5 percent, or almost one-third, of full-time employees had some type of flexible working hours.[1] Of course, most organizations experience occasions when employees need to work overtime, which can be disruptive to employees' personal lives. Administering time and a half overtime compensation in times of high-volume work is costly to departments with tight budgetary constraints and is something most administrators hope to avoid.

There are many types of flexible arrangements. These include:

- Flexible work schedules
- Non-traditional workweeks/compressed workweeks
- Split schedules
- Telecommuting from home or remote locations

1. United States Department of Labor, "Workers on Flexible and Shift Schedules in May 2004," news release, July 1, 2005, http://www.bls.gov/news.release/pdf/flex.pdf.

With some creativity and a keen eye on the policy manual for overtime obligations or special premiums, there are opportunities when work can be scheduled with a mutual benefit. As a reminder, by policy and by Fair Labor Standards Act regulations, overtime for non-exempt employees must be paid for work performed over forty hours in one week. A standard week begins at 12:00 a.m. on Sunday and ends at 11:59 p.m. on Saturday.[2]

Joe the Single Dad

Joe is a single dad with a daughter in kindergarten. Those of us who are parents know how difficult it may be to get our kids off to school and get to work on time. Joe starts work at nine and must get his daughter to school by eight thirty. Joe has been having difficulty getting to work on time and has been tardy four times in the last month.

Joe's boss can't permit Joe to be late for work with such regularity. He is a great employee, but he still can't be late when his coworkers must be on time. Joe talked to the boss about his daughter not wanting to leave him in the morning. He asked, "Can I work out a different schedule until I get this problem under control? What if I work from nine thirty to six thirty until I get this fixed? I really don't want to risk being disciplined for my tardiness."

---

2. Certain exceptions apply. Refer to the U.S. Department of Labor for details, especially for nursing and sales in particular. United States Department of Labor, "FairPay Fact Sheets by Occupation," http://www.dol.gov/esa/whd/regs/compliance/fairpay/fact_occupation.htm.

Well, what about it? Can you make an exception for Joe while the rest of the employees still have to be at work on time? Sure you can. In fact, pay close attention to employee hardships. You don't want to lose a great employee when you can make exceptions in cases like Joe's.

Of course, you may have coworkers who say, "Me too," but you need to look at the needs of your department. If you make an exception, say so; don't let the rumors fly. If others want an alternative schedule, create a policy that describes the possible arrangements.

Flexible Work Schedules

Flexible schedules can reflect many different types of arrangements. Starting and stopping times can vary within a "core business hours" schedule when all employees in a department are expected to be at work.

An example of this schedule:

Core business hours are nine to four. Some full-time employees have a choice within a two-hour period of when to start work. So, for example, an employee with a thirty-minute lunch break could work from seven to three thirty, seven thirty to four, eight to four thirty, or eight thirty to five. If the lunch break is sixty minutes, time would be adjusted to accommodate the additional thirty minutes.

If your department can accommodate a swing arrangement (meaning it would be at the employee's discretion to determine the start and end of each day), and the employee works the required amount of hours, then the employee can schedule personal obligations on off hours. One caution: though this arrangement provides the most flexibility for the employee, it is difficult to administer. Generally, with this type of scheduling, there is agreement in advance of what regular starting and stopping times will be.

Nontraditional Workweeks/Compressed Workweeks

Joe lives forty miles away from the office. Gas prices are on the rise, and he is worried that he can't afford to stay with the company. You can't afford to be without Joe; he is a well-valued cog in the workplace machine. You work with Joe to arrange for a compressed workweek. Let him work four days a week—it will work for you both.

A compressed workweek is a standard workweek that is shortened into fewer than five days. One common schedule is four ten-hour days per week (four-tens), like Joe works. By scheduling four-tens with staff working on different days of the week, such as schedules that include Mondays *or* Fridays off, work that extends into the evening hours can be done without the need for overtime coverage. Of course, the occasional need for overtime will arise, but on a routine basis, this type of schedule can be beneficial and responsive to both departmental and employee needs.

Should you make arrangements for a non-traditional workweek, you need to communicate with your payroll folks to prevent overtime payments from being applied to those employees.

Other types of schedules can be arranged such as nine-hour days on Monday through Thursday and a four-hour day on Friday. This schedule has been successfully managed in many organizations, particularly throughout the summer or off-season (a pilot of this type of program is recommended), to provide a longer weekend. Longer periods of coverage exist with this schedule for most of the week. It is recommended that the workweek revert to the traditional five-day schedule during weeks that include holidays, so that the appropriate amount of holiday pay is calculated.

Split Schedules

Joe is a trainer at a fitness center. They have such ebbs and flows of customers that the boss wants Joe to work a split schedule. Joe's schedule is 10:00 a.m. to 1:00 p.m. and 5:00 p.m. to 10:00 p.m. Great for the boss—he has coverage over a twelve-hour period—but this does not provide Joe with much of a personal life.

If you have a need to schedule work later in the day and have downtime earlier in the day, you should consider this type of split schedule. This type of schedule is a workday that is scheduled in two segments divided by a period exceeding one hour. You may need to provide a premium for a split schedule if there is a provision in your policies. This type of schedule could be your remedy to paying overtime for work beyond the end of the traditional quitting time without the expensive one and one-half times the regular rate of pay. Be advised that a split shift schedule is not very popular with employees, because they often complain of being always on the clock.

Telecommuting

Telecommuting can also work very well in some circumstances, but arrangements must be formalized. Employees may work from a remote location on one or more days per week, full-time, or only occasionally.

Telecommuting is *not* encouraged for non-exempt employees, but it can be done. Should this type of formalized scheduling arrangement occur, significant confidence and trust must exist between the manager and employee, along with careful documentation of actual working hours.

Some important principles apply to all types of telecommuting, whether formalized by specific agreement or occasional. While employees are working, whether on premises or not, they are covered under risk-management policies. Due to the fact that supervision is difficult from a remote location and an overriding principle is trust, off-site work should not be arranged for employees with performance deficiencies. When working off-site, the employee must commit to accomplishing their tasks, without distractions—such as caring for children—impeding their performance.

Relevant Questions to Consider

Did you ever "save" a good worker by being flexible in your scheduling? Was there a time when you lost a good employee because you did not have the ability to adapt to his or her needs? Think about how you may accommodate special needs and get better work out of your employees. Could you have saved money from your salary budget by using creative scheduling?

____

____

____

____

____

Chapter 8

Managing within the Confines of a Union Agreement

Joe the Union Member

If your staff is represented by a union, you will encounter unique challenges when managing and motivating them. There are many reasons for these challenges. In addition to a union's policies and standards that apply to the work area, there is also a collective bargaining agreement with provisions that are unique to the employment relationship. Supervisors must be aware of the unique nuances that apply to employees represented by a union. Further, there are limitations to recognition of good performance and work that is over and above the call of duty.

Think about fostering better and more productive relationships between you and your unionized staff within the confines of the collective bargaining agreement. While the union contract is limiting as to the wages and working conditions of the represented employee, there are ways you can successfully foster a sense of pride and ownership of the work product and create a more satisfying work environment overall. The subjects of bargaining include hiring issues, job pay and classification, job standards, and problem correction, including the administration of a progressive discipline philosophy.

Selection of Union Staff

Most collective bargaining agreements contain language that provides limitations on the selection and hiring process. For example, in the University of Michigan's (UM) agreement with American Federation of State, County and Municipal Employees (AFSCME), which represents wages and working conditions for service and maintenance employees, there is a provision that dictates that seniority is the determining factor for certain jobs:

> When the opening is filled, the employee with the most seniority among the bidders in the posting area who has the necessary qualifications will be given the promotion or transfer when the classification is assigned to pay grade 2 through 6. When the classification is assigned to pay grade 7 or above, qualifications shall be the determining factor, except that among those with equal qualifications seniority shall control.[1]

1. University of Michigan Human Resources, "AFSCME 2005 Contract," art. 20, sec. D, http://hr.umich.edu/staffhr/contracts/AFSCME2005contract.html.

According to this contract, the supervisor must consider a number of factors when selecting new employees. If the vacancy is assigned to the lower of the pay grade levels, the supervisor must put heavy weight on the bidder's seniority as it relates to other bidders. The language used in the agreement, however, clearly indicates that the successful bidder must have the necessary qualifications. In other words, careful attention must be paid to assure that the basic qualifications are met.

For example, a cook must have the basic proficiencies in the areas of reading and interpretation skills to follow a recipe. This includes measurement capabilities, or the understanding of fractions in weights and measures. If an employee with more seniority than the other bidders does not meet the basic qualifications that have been established by the supervisor, then the next bidder is considered. In other words, seniority rules for this level, but the successful candidate *still* must meet the basic, reasonable qualifications and proficiencies set forth for the position.

When there is a posted vacancy for a position that is assigned to a higher designated pay grade, the language provides much more selection power to the supervisor. For instance, a maintenance mechanic at a pay grade seven must first meet the qualifications for the position to be considered. The qualifications for this type of position typically include the ability to perform basic plumbing and electrical repair. There is nothing in this language that requires the supervisor to select a bidder internal to the organization prior to considering applicants outside of the bargaining unit. Seniority is a secondary determinant of the successful bidder in this case. If two top bidders have equal qualifications, then seniority is the determinant.

Even for union staff, supervisors should spend more time in the selection process. Of course, when there is a vacancy, most supervisors want to fill the vacancy in the swiftest manner possible. It's often difficult to wait for the process to finish. After all, the work must get done. It is time-consuming to create selection criteria, send the information for posting, review the bidders' information, interview, and select the appropriate candidate. When this process is rushed with a hasty selection, the supervisor often spends more time trying to remedy a bad hiring decision. The moral of the story is to take a step back and evaluate all of your options and make a fully informed hiring decision.

When selection criteria are established, they must be in keeping with the level of the position. They must meet the definition of a bona fide occupational qualification. If there is a vacancy for a cook, it is not essential that the candidate have a culinary arts degree. Of course, for a chef, that is a reasonable qualification, but it is not necessary for a cook who is following basic recipes.

In the interview process, it is important to fully describe the vacant position in appropriate detail. It is important to stress that pride and ownership of the work product is essential to the success of the department. Get some assurances from the bidders that they will support that philosophy. Make sure the prospective employee understands the particular demands for quality as well as the mission of the department.

Typical contract language includes the ability to return employees to a former classification if they don't have the ability to perform the duties of a position. Managers typically have one month to evaluate the skills and abilities of new employees, and if they are unable to perform in the new job, managers can return them to a position within their skill level. Remember, when employees interview for positions, they are presenting themselves in the best possible light. Sometimes inflated experience affects good hiring decisions.

Pride and Ownership of the Work Product

An employee's pride and ownership of the work product *always* results in better performance and productivity. The issue of how to foster this pride with a union staff often creates a challenge for supervision. Why is this? It's this simple: employees who do repetitive duties, and perform work at the service and maintenance level, often expect to be assigned a set of responsibilities and are not asked for input. They are trained and expected to perform to the specifications that their supervisor provides. It is more difficult for them to take pride in their work without participation.

Supervisors often ask about ways to motivate their union employees within the confines of the labor agreement. The answer lies within the agreement itself, but remember that the union agreement is "limiting," as opposed to "permitting."

Joe the Supervisor of Union Staff

Joe is the manager of a performing arts complex in a county government. He supervises both union and non-union employees. He often provides complimentary concert tickets to events as a perquisite to his staff. But Joe has a problem; he can't give tickets to the union employees. How can the non-union employees in his department get more benefits than the county's union employees? If Joe denies the union staff equal perks, are they polarized? Do they feel less valued than the rest of the staff? Yes, indeed.

Because I was their human resource consultant, Joe contacted me. He complained, "I wish the union contract permitted me to give them tickets." When I responded with "What in this agreement *prohibits* you from giving them tickets?" it forced us to look closer at the agreement. First and foremost, labor unions operate under the mantra of the Three Musketeers: "All for one, and one for all." With this overriding philosophy in mind, we had to be careful about providing only a dozen employees in one department with an incredible perk, and not all 1,000 union members in the entire county.

The resolution to this issue is very telling. On one hand, the employees were part of the department. They functioned alongside the rest of the performing arts staff. On the other hand, they were represented by the union that negotiated their wages and monitored their working conditions. We held a meeting with the union to come to a resolution. We explained to the union leadership that we viewed the perk as a recognition of the employees' hard work and that singling out the non-union employees in the department would create an "us vs. them" mentality. They agreed to make an exception to their policies, and the union members within the department received their tickets.

We made a special agreement with the union that arranged for unique circumstances specific to departmental needs. By providing this agreement for this specific circumstance, there was no violation of the union contract. This was achieved by positive communication and a constructive compromise with the union leadership.

Joe the Baker

Joe is a baker in a catering business. He is the only baker and is seriously overworked. When Joe tried to talk to his boss about his demanding schedule, he was told, "Sorry, nothing I can do about it. Just get 'er done." Little did the boss know, Joe had ideas about how he could streamline his work and get everything done.

Joe burned a whole order of brownies because he was pulled in every direction doing other duties. The company lost time and money.

What can a tray of burned brownies do to a food service organization? If the food is substandard, the business will suffer. It's that simple. How about the supervisor who works on ways to foster employee pride and ownership in their food service products? She listens to the employees' ideas on how to do the job better. Some ideas for consideration for workplace efforts include informal recognition for jobs well done. Since the entire staff is involved in creating the product, be careful to involve all levels of employees in the decision-making process. The staff will take complaints regarding the food very seriously and become involved in problem correction. This is done in a corrective, not punitive, mode. There is no finger-pointing here.

After all, isn't the success of an organization dependent upon the performance and success of the employees doing the work? Feedback and participation in the day-to-day operations of an organization by all facets of the workforce are essential. That's if an organization views people as their greatest asset. Many organizations claim that they follow this concept, but in order to really live this idea, supervisors need to take the following issues into consideration:

- Do they hire and train the right people for the right job? Without a solid and well-trained workforce, it is difficult to view their people as their greatest asset. After all, how can supervisors expect pride and ownership in a work product without these essential principles?
- Do they motivate and recognize employees? Keep in mind that motivation and recognition of employees is a universal principle. Don't leave the unionized employee out in the cold, without recognition. Remember, without recognition it is unlikely that employees will contribute new ideas and take pride in their work.

- Are they learning the *expectation*, as opposed to the status quo? Learning begins with the individual, but that is only the beginning. If an organization is to grow and learn, learning experiences must be shared with others in the team or the organization. Positive feedback is expected and problems are considered as learning experiences.

Relevant Questions to Consider

Do you manage in a union environment where you have concerns about motivating and rewarding the union employees? Think about ways to work with the union employees to create a more productive work environment. Do you involve them in discussions regarding better ways to get the work done? Union members want to contribute to the success of your department. Just ask them.

____

____

____

____

____

Union Avoidance

Many, many managers have asked about how they can avoid a union-organizing campaign in their workplace. The answer is pretty simple: keep employees happy, and understand their needs.

A relative's unpopular boyfriend asked me, "How can I get my girlfriend's mother to like me?" I responded quickly, "Treat her daughter right!" The same principle applies here. If employees feel that they are treated well and are given a fair shake, they will not care about paying union dues to someone to watch out for them. Treat them right and communicate.

As one late union leader said, "Treat employees right, follow the rules, keep them updated about company issues, and you won't have to deal with a union."

At one public company, not only were we eager to remain union-free, we wanted to survey our staff to find out what made them tick. Our turnover was out of control, and we needed to get a handle on the employees' priorities and their ideas on ways to make their workplace better. Upon analysis of the survey results, we realized that there were a number of excellent points discovered in the survey. The staff requested access to tuition refund, flexible schedules, and fair approval of time off. We also knew that we could not accomplish all of the reasonably requested changes in a short time frame.

Instead of sending the results in the form of a memo, we created a program for a staff meeting so we could report a summary of the results and ask for the staff's participation in prioritizing the ideas. The program was called "You asked; we listened." It was wildly successful. Not only was the staff able to see the results, they understood how they could assist in making the organization better by prioritizing the requested changes. The staff was also told which of their ideas were not possible, such as an immediate raise in pay. Though we couldn't implement that idea immediately, we provided our plan for salary improvement over the next two years, should the organization yield expected profits. The staff's participation yielded much more excitement than was expected from the survey. Involvement and understanding is critical for employees to feel ownership of their jobs.

If you find yourself in a union-organizing campaign, don't panic and certainly don't stop communicating to the staff. Many employers hire skilled consultants to assist them with this process. There is a danger of unfair labor practices occurring during a campaign, which you won't want to deal with.

Take a look at the National Labor Relations Act web site, listed in the Recommended Readings and Web Sites section at the back of this book. Know your rights during a union-organizing campaign. For the most part, union organizers are not permitted to organize in your workplace during working hours, nor are they permitted on your property. In many, if not most, circumstances, the organizers are employees in your organization. In this case, you can prohibit discussions about an organizing campaign during working hours.

Tell your employees the truth about issues raised by union organizers. If *they* are not being truthful, it is your right to let the employees know the real deal. It is perfectly legal to communicate to your employees.

Chapter 9

Compensation and Job Titles

A formal promotion is not always necessary to recognize an employee's achievements and duties. Depending on organizational rules concerning pay and classification, changes in an employee's responsibilities can be recognized by a new job code, working title, or pay adjustment.

On a day-to-day basis, employees don't require a formal title change to receive meaningful recognition, particularly when tough times leave you with no options for additional monetary compensation. Alternative methods can be used to compensate, classify, and recognize employees, without promoting them. Options for recognizing staff with additional pay include a one-time lump sum payment, special payments, and temporary paid assignments.

Compensation for Additional Effort of Exempt Employees

Exempt employees are not entitled to overtime compensation. However, at the discretion of your organization, there may be an occasional opportunity to provide extra compensation to exempt employees for their efforts. This compensation can be provided for various reasons, including special initiatives that require significantly more time and effort on an employee's part. This could include the exempt employee who volunteers for weekend duties, accomplishes a special project, or performs additional work to meet a deadline.

Compensation can be provided for additional effort at the department's discretion, in the form of special payment (in either hours or lump sum) or additional vacation time/ paid time off (PTO).

Temporary Promotion

You may have an occasional need to provide additional compensation to employees who temporarily increase their responsibilities.

If this is the case, ask yourself:

- How is the nature of the temporary work different from the employee's regular work?
- Is there a significant difference in the new responsibilities that would necessitate recognition in pay?

- How long will this temporary work be assigned?
- Will these new responsibilities be necessary for at least three months?
- Is this an increase in *volume* of work or in *scope* of work?

If an employee is just doing a higher volume of work, as opposed to a higher level of work, you can provide additional compensation in recognition of the work, but should not provide a temporary promotion.

If the nature of a work assignment significantly changes during a fixed period of time, such as three to six months as acting manager of a department, a temporary promotion is an appropriate option.

You can compensate employees for temporary promotions by a lump sum payment or a special increase to their base salary for a specified period of time. Be sure to provide realistic time frames and be open to time extensions if necessary.

Methods for processing pay increases for temporary promotions include submitting a pay increase on whichever type of pay change form your organization uses along with a temporary title change. This formal recognition of the pay and title change provides substantiation for the future. You never know when the boss or auditors will come knocking for information to support your staff changes.

Salary Adjustments for Market and/or Internal Pay Relationship Changes

Adjustments to pay may be necessary due to changes in the job market or conditions affecting internal pay relationships. These adjustments may be necessary for recruitment, retention, and maintenance of appropriate pay relationships within a department.

Salary Adjustments in Recognition of Additional Duties

Should a staff member be assigned additional responsibilities without the majority of their responsibilities changing, consider providing an administrative differential. In this case, a change in job code is not necessary. An additional funding line can be added on a data submittal form to facilitate this change.

Salary Adjustments for Exceptional Performance

At a department's discretion, a midyear increase can be processed either for employees who are exhibiting exceptional performance, or to level salaries. Midyear pay adjustments are additions to the base salary and are not a part of the annual salary program.

Ways to compensate for a midyear pay adjustment include providing the employee with a lump sum payment that does not build upon the base salary or an increase to the compensation rate that will build on base salary. Remember if you provide an increase to the base salary, normally it remains there and future increases are calculated on the new amount.

There is a rule of thumb that nonmonetary recognition is more meaningful to the employee. In my experience, that has rarely been the case. Though a simple thank you or public acknowledgement of a job well done goes a long way, most of the employees I know would like more money at the end of the workday.

Relevant Questions to Consider

In times of financial belt-tightening, how do you reward employees who go beyond the call of duty? Do nonmonetary rewards become more important? What type of reward systems do you have in place or plan to initiate?

____

____

____

____

____

Joe the Wannabe

"Hey, that's my job title. Why are you using it?" Joe's boss asked. Joe was calling himself "department manager" when in fact, he was a team leader. Joe's boss—the department's actual manager—took offense to this and corrected Joe, much to Joe's embarrassment. Joe took job title liberties that ended in admonishment.

Employees take pride in what they are called, both on and off the job. For many, it is often more important than their pay. Use the following overriding principles and your organization will understand the all-important pecking order. What's in a title? Plenty!

Overriding Principles of Creating Job Titles:

- Identify a job title structure that will define the parameters of management designations.
- Be consistent when assigning titles.
- Make sure the title accurately reflects responsibilities.
- Provide clear career direction.
- Use titles that are consistent with the market.

Excellent working titles should:

- clarify management roles;
- convey appropriate message to the outside world;
- identify with the outside market;
- be able to be used for clearer definition in organizational directories;
- identify correct role on business cards;
- identify the right parties on web site(s).

A working title should not be used when there is an official organizational title of the same name. Further, and critically, a working title should not misrepresent the authority or function of the position.

Definitions of Management Positions

It is best to establish unmistakable leadership titles that define their roles well. This provides clear definition of authority, both to employees inside and to clients outside of the organization. The information that follows includes universally recognized management levels and their typical lines of authority.

Senior-Level Director Line Definitions

Executive Director

Directs long-range strategic planning, and operational and/or marketing activities of several divisions. Provides vision of the area of supervision and implements the vision organization-wide.

Senior Director

Plans and directs administrative and operational activities with broad, cross-functional responsibility for several divisions.

Director

Serves as administrator of a division and/or function with broad responsibility. Assumes full financial and operational accountability and directs multiple levels of employees.

Director Line Definitions

Associate Director

Provides comprehensive management assistance to the director in all aspects of the division's operations. May act as director in periods of absence.

Assistant Director

Provides management assistance to the director in one or more aspects of the division's operations. May act as director in periods of absence.

Manager

Manages support staff in a functional department. Assumes the responsibility of creating and monitoring departmental objectives, evaluating employee performance, setting priorities, assigning tasks, and managing the assigned budget and other resources to accomplish departmental objectives.

Manager Line Definitions

Assistant Manager

Generally provides guidance to first-line supervisors by reviewing performance evaluations and performance standards, and by assisting with departmental budget.

Manager of Projects/Programs

Manages all aspects of a project or program that may or may not involve the administrative supervision of staff.

Operations Manager

Represents management and coordinates budgets, logistical issues, and a department's business functions.

Supervisor

Supervises employees in a functional and/or administrative capacity with moderate authority to make decisions and is held accountable for results. Assumes the authority to recommend hires, give evaluations, discipline, dispense pay, and/or assign work.

Coordinator

Coordinates the organization and dissemination of information, programs, and projects. Functional coordination over work assignments may be exercised.

Relevant Questions to Consider

Take a look at the titles of your staff. Do they fit into your organizational structure? Are they significantly "out of sync" with the market? If so, what are your plans to review and correct?

____

____

____

____

____

Chapter 10

How Do I Measure Success?

Your boss wants metrics. How you measure the success of your employees is a hot topic. Their success gives you credibility in your boss's eyes. Remember that your leaders want data, and a lack of analytical information can harm you. Be ready.

Some think the term "metrics" is a four-letter word. Let's discuss how metrics, or measurements of the activities of your employee, can be managed in a simple method. Metrics need not intimidate you—they can make you a management superstar.

Joe the Unemployed

Pat was asked by the hearing officer at the unemployment compensation hearing, "What did you not like about Joe's performance?"

After a brief silence, Pat responded, "Well, there were problems that other administrators told me about." What *others* said? What about Pat's personal measurements of dissatisfaction with Joe? She didn't have any. Were there any performance measurements in place or was this information contrived by others?

You need to know how to measure levels of satisfaction with an employee's job performance. Measuring the activity of your staff allows you to create a comfort zone in which you can identify issues necessitating change or areas needing enhanced communication.

Has your manager ever come to you to ask for a status report concerning a topic when you don't have the data at your fingertips? It sure has happened to me, and it's not pretty if you can't provide that information in quick order.

Let's talk about how to be ready. First of all, what can you learn and achieve by analysis of trends? Your metrics. Trends simply tell a story about how you and your staff are performing. Your advance preparation provides you with a template for succession planning when there is turnover. Of course, the issues vary based upon your business, but the principles are the same.

Identify your stakeholders. Some stakeholders are obvious: your boss, senior leadership, and your customers. Less obvious stakeholders include colleagues in other departments who count on your services and anyone else who may rely on your services. You need to know if your customers' needs are being met. We all have customers whether we work in sales, education, or public service. Always, and I mean *always*, measure customer feedback. Survey at least once a year to keep your finger on the pulse of the receivers of your service. Customer feedback is a gift.

Rank the importance of critical feedback. It will help you determine the significance of your measures. For example, your measurement of turnover may not be as critical as productivity.

Look at job satisfaction. I think satisfied employees produce good work, which in turn makes *you* look good. Right? And with feedback, you know who is satisfied, and who is not.

Ask yourself, *Have the employees reached their goals? Were the goals achievable? Reasonable?* Look to see what makes sense. Rank your essential staff. We are all replaceable, but who would cause the most stress on your department if he or she were to leave? In other words, who are your superstars and who can you do without? Ask your staff to list special initiatives they are working on. Do they readily volunteer? Do they seek out work that will enhance their value? Is the return on performance and service equal to your expectations? Are you getting the bang for the buck?

Analyze your turnover, and analyze again! Keep a running list of employees who have left your employ. Keep track of the reasons why the position turned over, noting the position title, its department, and the job description. It is very costly to lose staff. One good estimate from the Society for Human Resource Management (SHRM) is that it costs at least $3,500 to replace an employee paid just over minimum wage. This includes costs of recruiting, interviewing, training, and potential overtime for others.

Other estimates of cost range from 30 percent to 50 percent of the annual salary, and 150 percent to 400 percent for highly specialized employees.[1] Though this figure varies wildly based upon the type of business and employee, the point is that turnover is expensive and time-consuming.

There are online worksheets that you can use to determine more exact costs of employee turnover. They are available on the SHRM web site. There are also free materials available from the Department of Labor.

Make sure that you are paying your staff appropriately considering the market for the position, balanced by your ability to pay. Perhaps your organization cannot offer pay consistent with the market, but you can create a compensation philosophy that describes your financial capability. You can make a determination for each position about whether you will *lead* or *lag* market pay, according to market conditions. You can obtain market salary information from numerous associations such as WorldatWork or the Society for Human Resource Management, or from a reputable compensation consulting firm, such as Watson Wyatt, Sibson Consulting, or Tandehill Human Capital.

1. Ross Blake, "Employee Retention: What Employee Turnover Really Costs You,"WebProNews, http://www.webpronews.com/expertarticles/2006/07/24/employee-retention-what-employee-turnover-really-costs-your-company.

If you neglect to keep your eye on where the salaries of your staff fall within the market, you will likely have turnover and will have to pay a higher pay rate for new recruits. This is particularly difficult in hard economic times. Be realistic, and communicate with your staff about your ability to pay.

Take a look at the relative importance of staff and their titles. Many of us, if not most, base our professional value on our job titles. Evaluate the titles of your staff and make sure there is a logical progression of the titles. Lack of attention to this detail results in confusion of roles and potential problems with morale.

Measure the reasons for your loss of employees. There is much debate about the value of exit interviews, but the information they provide is better than none at all. Create an online exit interview that zeros in on the issues that are important to your business. Though you can't expect full honesty, these results will give you insight into issues you may not know about.

If you see a trend or metric that you should evaluate further, be sure to do so. Make sure you look into potential problem correction, and facilitate group discussions to solicit advice on room for improvement in a benign manner.

Refer to www.managementexperienceacquired.com for a helpful tool that you can use to start your process of measuring the success of your staff.

Relevant Questions to Consider

What type of measurement tools do you use? Have your been caught unprepared when the boss asked for information concerning your metrics? What is your plan to be prepared?

____

____

____

____

____

Chapter 11

Evaluate Them Right

Joe the Stunned

Joe was quite anxious. His meeting to discuss his annual performance evaluation had been scheduled. He was afraid to hear his boss's comments, primarily because he hadn't had any conversations or received any feedback about his performance since last year. He didn't know if the boss was keeping statistics on his progress. He had no advance work plan or expectations. Nothing.

The boss sat down with Joe and described a whole litany of issues with his performance. Dumbfounded, Joe listened and responded with a puzzled look that the boss took as a lack of cooperative attitude, despite the fact that Joe was the most respected employee of the bunch and produced the best work.

These are all too common problems in the workplace: lack of clearly defined expectations and objectives, and no regular feedback. The result of these problems is the potential loss of a great employee.

Commonly, bosses feel consternation about the evaluation process. Which format should I use? How should I involve employees? Should I do one at all? Most organizations have a performance appraisal process for managers to follow and there are many excellent systems out there that assist the boss with the process. No matter which process or system is used, there are principles to follow that will make the experience more meaningful and useful.

There is a school of thought that performance appraisals are out of style and inhibit productivity. A variation of the traditional appraisal process results in considerable improvement in value. A work plan that is agreed upon at the beginning of the review period provides a good plan for employee involvement and clarification of expectations.

Create a work plan with the employee and make sure he participates in the development of the plan. Let him have the autonomy to perform his job within the parameters that meet your comfort level. Further, you need a tool to evaluate performance that mirrors the work plan. This is a perfect solution.

Create the model employee. Show your staff what a picture of success looks like.

Joe's boss had a secret stash of performance expectations. He didn't involve the employees in goal setting, but he always had his handy clipboard with him to write down his observations of the staff. When the boss was in the workplace, whispers erupted. "Shh, he's here!"

Well, this boss managed an auditing function. Much to the surprise of the audit staff, his expectation was that they audit at least seventy invoices per day. Some auditors were dropping like flies, and no one knew why. Others were promoted to senior-level positions because of their accuracy and speed. The boss needed to tell them what good performance looked like, but never did. For him, a good performance entailed:

- auditing at least seventy invoices per day;
- maintaining a solid working knowledge of clients;
- creating status reports;
- always being at your desk at 8:00 a.m.;
- being available for customer calls and returning calls promptly.

I recall a time when I didn't have a clue if I was performing up to a boss's standards. I did my work to my personal best, but doubted whether the boss liked my work. It was only when I overheard a conversation wherein the boss raved about my performance that I had a grounded view of my performance and the confidence to thrive.

First of all, involve your employee in the evaluation process from the very beginning. Explain what is expected and get agreement on what will be evaluated. Any system permits a sit-down with employees at the beginning of the review period to set expectations, whether this step is included in the formal process or not. If you have an agreed upon work plan, your job will be easier because the expectations are "front-loaded." Use the responsibilities of his job that are typically found on a job description as a guide to create goals for the next review period.

Agree on goals and objectives, a work plan, and expected dates of completion and measurement. Completion dates can be amended during update meetings.

There are fine performance appraisal systems available, such as the Performance Impact system, which provides language you can use in the performance evaluation process. Performance Impact provides for employee self-evaluation as a starting point to the review. Reluctantly, I used the system and quickly grew to admire its value.

In preparation for performance appraisals:

1. For your eyes only, rank your staff in relative value and importance of role. (Consistent with your ongoing measurements.) You know how to do this. Think about how your employees perform on a regular basis; you know who is performing well and who is not.

2. Keep an ongoing file of particularly good and remarkably substandard incidents of performance for each employee. Create usable observations, not generalizations. This will make your task much simpler at review time.
3. Look at the standards that you have set in your area of control. Does your staff understand the standards? Do you feel comfortable with the expectations? If not, revise the standards and include employees in the conversation.
4. Carefully prepare your conversation in advance. Don't present an ill-informed evaluation. Remember, many employees may not admit to their shortcomings or take responsibility for their actions.
5. When preparing for delicate conversations, outline not only the facts of the problem, but how to agreeably resolve it. Often, employees don't know how to fix the problem. Help them.
6. Think about succession planning. Is there growth potential for your employees? What would it take for them to get there? Discuss the potentials and visit the possibility of assistance for advancement.
7. Have your employees perform a self-assessment prior to your evaluation. It's a great tool and can be a real eye-opener. Remember, you can't be everywhere at all times. Most employees will be modest in a self-evaluation.

8. Remember, the performance appraisal process is *not* discipline. Discipline may follow or parallel the appraisal process. The process is intended to provide goals, objectives, and feedback concerning general performance.

First and foremost, a performance evaluation should never be a surprise to your employees. Feedback, good or bad, should continue throughout the year. When there is the element of surprise at appraisal time, there has been a breakdown in communication.

Always take the time to discuss your employee's plans and goals within your organization. Make it a part of your performance evaluation process. He may be happy to remain in his job, or perhaps his career aspirations will take him to a galaxy far, far away. Whatever the case, you need to know his plans. Is there something you can do to assist him in reaching his goals? Will he help your company adapt to change? You may find that you have a diamond in the rough who is destined to become a superstar with a little assistance and grooming.

Joe the Immobile

Don't assume that everyone is upwardly mobile or wants to be. Joe was a secretary who did a great job and was very smart at diagnosing problems in his department. His boss, Ann, assumed that everyone had the same high career aspirations as she did, and recommended that Joe take some accounting classes to ready himself for his next promotion. Joe responded that he was in a place in his life where he wanted to focus on creating artwork. He had no higher-level goals at Ann's company. He just wanted to work eight hours a day, leave work on his desk for the night, and spend his evening working on his craft.

Does that make Joe an unmotivated employee? Or does that just make him different? Don't get caught up in thinking everyone has the same career goals. Managers often evaluate employees based on their own aspirations. Be careful; Joe could be doing an excellent job with the duties that he is assigned.

Joe the Consummate Gofer

Joe is your management trainee. He is always happy to go for this, go for that. He is very cooperative. In fact, he is the most qualified trainee you have. But when it comes to the guts of the work, Joe is always busy with the basic work and shows neither initiative nor progress. You wonder about his aspirations. Does Joe want to grow, or is he happy just doing the basic work?

We all play the role of gofer at some point in our careers; it's part of the game of gaining experience. We try to please the people who matter, and we graciously do the mundane things well. But beware of becoming the consummate gofer. If your desire is to be upwardly mobile, make your aspirations clear. Do you know workplace gofers who stay in jobs that lead nowhere? If that is their desire, then fine. But if you aspire for bigger and better things, watch the branding that comes with this label.

Joe the Blindsided

Joe was conducting his first report using Sarbanes-Oxley statistical reporting standards. He was satisfied with his results, verified the information, and was ready to submit the information. He then discovered that the report could not be submitted due to a password problem. Joe thought, *No worries, there are two weeks left until the due date.* He talked to his boss, Mary Jane, who claimed to understand that Joe had everything under control.

Joe continued to attempt to submit the report with no success. Mary Jane didn't care to assist. After working with the state, Joe finally got the password and successfully submitted the report two days after the deadline. Joe was relieved he finished.

In a conversation with Mary Jane, Joe told her of his success submitting the report. Her response? "Keep good records on this so when I put negative comments on your performance appraisal, you may be able to defend yourself. You were late."

"What? I just explained what happened," said Joe. Dazed and confused, Joe got to work on his job search. He knew that as long as Mary Jane was there, he had no future with the organization. Obviously, Mary Jane was not fit to manage. Joe resigned, and the company soon realized that Mary Jane was the problem. Shortly thereafter, Mary Jane suddenly left the organization.

Sure, none of us likes delivering bad news, but a problem usually does not go away on its own. Think about a time when your delay in working on the problem made it worse. What would you do differently next time?

Bad news is tough to deliver, but catastrophic news is worse. If you think that coddling your employee is better medicine than being honest with him, think again. Don't avoid unflattering feedback; the alternative is much worse. Enable him to correct the ills of his performance before it's too late; don't let him wallow in a comfort zone that doesn't exist. Otherwise, by the time your employee realizes that he is in hot water, he may not be able to sustain employment. Evaluate employees often, and give them current feedback.

One Employer's Creative Approach to Post-Evaluation Problems

If employees are not meeting expectations, and have an overall unacceptable performance appraisal score (based on your standards and rating scale), provide them with detailed information outlining the correction necessary to remain employed. In this case, this level of generally unsatisfactory performance automatically places an employee in the status of "further performance review required."

The supervisor will be responsible for holding ongoing review meetings with the employee for up to forty-five days. Progress must be monitored to see if there is a possibility of problem correction. Remember, if employees are designated "immediate improvement necessary" from an overall performance standpoint, there are serious problems they need to correct in order for them to remain employed.

If employees are having difficulty performing a job, the ongoing review is a good mechanism to identify and correct problems Remember, this is not part of the discipline process but a performance improvement plan.

While the performance appraisal provides an evaluation of expected competencies, the ongoing review needs to outline for the employee the specific job responsibilities needing *immediate* correction. The role of the supervisor is to help employees meet that requirement.

- First, establish the area of concern. Be specific about the performance problems. What exactly is wrong? Discuss the details of the problem.
- Attempt to have the employee agree on the problem. This substantiates the need for correction and involves the employee in discussions about improvement. If that's not possible, the employee needs to know that the specific issues need to be immediately corrected.
- Listen to any mitigating factors that the employee brings to your attention. These excuses could have merit.
- Agree on the approach to fix the problem, and attempt to eliminate it.

- Follow up on your actions and don't lock yourself into keeping the employee in the position indefinitely. During the forty-five-day period, status meetings are important. You are *not* required to wait forty-five days to take action if it is clear that the employee:

- Does not have the capability to correct the problems
- Does not have the interest or attitude necessary to correct the problems
- Does not maintain the necessary quality of work or quality is regressing

Relevant Questions to Consider

Evaluate your performance appraisal process. Do you involve your employees in the goals and objectives process? Do you maintain records of observations of both positive and negative performance? What can you do to foster more employee participation? Do you provide periodic updates on employees' progress? Are you on the road to becoming a gofer or do you supervise any gofers?

____

____

____

____

____

Chapter 12

Problem Employees

Joe the War Hero

Joe was a decorated war hero whom everyone recognized. He was also an usher in a performing arts theater, and his job was to handle crowd control to make sure the show started on time. He was known for his lack of customer service skills. He was often cranky and didn't understand the word "finesse." From his perspective, he had a job to do, and nobody would stand in his way.

Well, Joe had quite the reputation for yelling at patrons, including the local elite. Complaints had been brought to his boss, and Joe had been warned about the consequences of his behavior. Joe didn't take it very seriously. After all, he was "Joe the War Hero." Everyone admired him. Joe could do no wrong! In reality, he had more chances than most employees could ever expect. Coworkers said, "That Joe can do anything. If I behaved that way, I would be out on my ear." The boss had considered mitigating circumstances to the point of being unproductive to the business.

"How much weight do you place on mitigating circumstances?" is a common question that managers have asked me. Of course, there is no magic formula, but the answer lies in how you explain the difference in treatment or the diversion from the rules. What is your own comfort level? What is your gut feeling? Your intuition provides a starting point for making your decision. I have often recommended that managers "sleep on" their decisions. Letting the issue steep creates stronger insight into your correct course of action.

If patrons, coworkers, or your boss say to you, "Hey, why do you permit this employee to damage our business?" then you need to remove the problem, regardless of any special circumstances surrounding the employee. *That* is the limit of your comfort level.

When the time comes to follow corrective discipline with an employee, follow these general principles.

Progressive and corrective discipline requires a commitment to do the job well. On more than one occasion, managers have asked me when they can go to the next step immediately following a step of corrective discipline. Give your employee a chance to fix their mistakes and perform well.

Whenever decisions are made concerning disciplinary action, it is important to remember that the burden of proof is squarely on the organization. When discipline is appealed, it typically comes in the form of a grievance and/

or arbitration, or from an outside agency, such as the U.S. Equal Employment Opportunity Commission (EEOC). The challenge falls clearly on the shoulders of the supervisor involved in the disciplinary action and the witnesses to the events that led to the disciplinary action.

Arbitrators and judges absolutely expect proof of some sort of progressive discipline, notice, or clear standards. Unless there is a significant event that would lead to immediate discharge, such as theft or violence, there is an expectation that there has been some progressive, corrective action taken prior to the termination of employment.

Supervisors must first determine why there is a problem occurring in the workplace with the employee. The supervisor should not make an automatic assumption that misconduct has occurred.

Misconduct is defined as the willful disregard of the interests of the employer. Typical types of misconduct include unexcused absenteeism (including tardiness), negligent work performance, insubordination, theft, threats, and inappropriate behavior on the job.

Options for the supervisor to administer corrective and progressive discipline are listed on page 101. Those are common types of discipline that are recognized by most employers and unions. We need to remember that for each case of misconduct, not all of the steps of corrective discipline need to be followed.

While some progressive discipline is recommended for most cases, all cases must be treated individually. There are rarely two cases of discipline with the exact same circumstances. All employees have different seniority and different records of performance. For this reason, we need to treat everyone in the workplace *equitably*, not equally. Equitable treatment means that the supervisor shall consider all of the factors concerning the case, any aggravating circumstances (facts that are unfavorable for the employee), and any mitigating circumstances (facts that are favorable for the employee).

For example, a supervisor may give an employee who is regularly tardy, has six months of service with the employer, and has a record of verbal warnings, a written warning for a certain infraction, while another employee with five years of service and a clean work record may receive a lesser form of corrective action under very similar circumstances. In essence, this is not "equal" treatment but "equitable" treatment.

Joe the Custodian

When a problem is identified, it could also be as the result of an inability to perform the responsibilities of the job. This is demonstrated by the following example:

Years ago, I was contacted by a supervisor who had concerns about the performance of an employee with ten years of seniority as a Custodian I, the first-level custodial worker. His regular responsibilities included sweeping, dusting, and picking up trash.

Joe, the custodian, applied for and was awarded a higher-level custodial position. One of the responsibilities of this new position included operating a floor buffer. The floor buffer was a rather large piece of equipment, particularly when compared to Joe, who was barely five feet tall and less than one hundred pounds.

The supervisor was getting complaints from building occupants about the quality of Joe's floor care. He automatically assumed that Joe was being negligent in his responsibilities and contacted me about disciplining Joe for his misconduct. When I reviewed the case, it was discovered that Joe had been a dedicated and responsible employee with a flawless personnel file.

When we looked deeper into the situation, we discovered that Joe had a problem operating the floor buffer. It wasn't a misconduct case at all, but an inability to perform in the higher-level position. Remember the Peter Principle? Had we not reviewed all of the facts concerning the case, Joe would have been given disciplinary action for misconduct. Finding a position for him in his former classification solved the problem.

Don't automatically assume your employee should be disciplined for misconduct. He may just be unable to perform the responsibilities of the job.

This remedy not only met the satisfaction of the supervisor, but Joe and his union as well. I saved this employee from disciplinary action by looking under the surface. Joe remains a good employee to this day.

Okay, you have done due diligence to *hire* a good candidate, you have *oriented* the employee well, and you have *trained* the new employee, providing a good workplace mentor. As a manager, these are your "HOT" areas: Hiring, Orienting, and Training. If there is a breakdown in any one of these three areas, you will likely have a problem with the employment relationship.

When you come to the realization that there is a problem with an employee, examine these issues. Take a look at the possibility that the wrong person is in the job. Ask yourself, *Does the employee have the qualifications that he identified on his resume? Did he embellish his experience? Is he the right person for the job he is doing?*

Next, examine the orientation you provided your employee. Was he given the right introduction to the organization, and particularly to his own work area?

Once again, review the employee's training and mentoring. Was there something missing that could have prevented the performance difficulties he's exhibiting? Look closely at the areas of concern and review the training and grooming initiatives that were provided.

If you discover a breakdown in any step of the hiring and grooming process, take a step back, reorient, and retrain. Maybe you hired someone without the full complement of skills and abilities that you expected. In that case, examine whether the employee should remain employed.

After you have reviewed the HOT issues and feel comfortable with the results of your employee's status, take a look at the root of the problem. You need to decide whether the problem is *misconduct* or *inability to perform*. The method of handling the problem will differ depending on its cause.

Let's look at the issue of misconduct first. Remember, if your employee is exhibiting a willful disregard of your workplace—misconduct—he should be subject to corrective and progressive discipline.

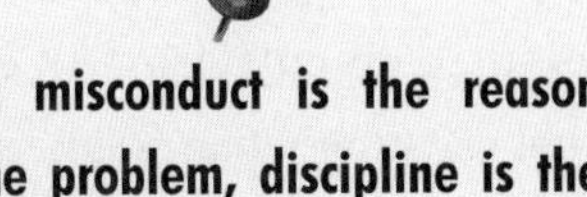

Misconduct includes but is not limited to:

- Insubordination
- Unexcused absenteeism and chronic tardiness
- Negligent work performance
- Threats and fighting
- Disruption to the workplace
- Theft
- Conflict of Interest

Remember, you need to think about what is the appropriate action. The level of seriousness of the problem needs to be established to determine the level of disciplinary action. For example, if your employee is chronically tardy or exhibiting negligence on the job, you would want to use progressive and corrective discipline.

Corrective and progressive discipline is a process wherein the expectation is that the employee will correct the problem, and no further discipline is necessary. If the employee fails, the expectation is that the discipline will progress further. This type of discipline is commonly used with unexcused absenteeism. An employee will typically receive a verbal warning when frequently tardy, absent from the work area without an excuse, or fails to follow call-in procedures. Should this problem persist, a written warning would follow, and possibly a final warning letter, which would serve as the last opportunity to correct the problem.

On the flip side, if your employee was stealing from the organization, you would not provide him with another opportunity to refrain from theft. You would want to immediately remove him from your workplace. The same thing applies for threats, fighting, and gross refusal to perform work assignments.

Insubordination in the workplace is the refusal to perform a work directive.

Simply, if Joe was unable to perform, you would not want to give him disciplinary action, but instead, would want to correct the workplace problem. Remember the case of Joe the Custodian who did not have the capability to perform the higher-level job? You need to correct the problem using methods such as a job relocation, position reassignment, and search assistance, while providing a time frame for ending employment as the employee searches for a job elsewhere. When you have exhausted methods of assistance to Joe, termination or offer of resignation may be the final option.

Employees who are given *reasonable* work orders and refuse the assignment, are committing acts of insubordination. Behaviors that magnify and aggravate insubordination include showing attitude, swearing, yelling, etc.

Can employees legitimately refuse work orders? There are a few reasons you must consider when evaluating the possibility of insubordination:

Does the employee have the ability to perform the assignment?

Chances are the employee has the skills but perhaps not the depth expected for the assignment. For example, you may have hired a skilled administrative assistant who is a whiz at most computer applications, but who doesn't have the depth of knowledge to perform sophisticated Excel calculations.

Does the employee think the assignment is a conflict of interest or includes ethical concerns?

If the employee claims a conflict of interest, think carefully about the allegation. If you have asked the employee to do personal work for you, either for an outside business or private business, think again. This is of particular concern when you work for a public employer. If you want your employee to drive your children to football practice, think again.

Is the duty unsafe?

This is an area where I have seen employees astutely refuse assignments. Case in point: a group of employees came to my office one afternoon refusing an assignment. Their supervisor had given them a work directive to clean offices in a building that was infested with pigeon droppings. When the employees refused, they were threatened with discipline for insubordination. When the problem was investigated, it was determined that they did not have the proper breathing protection necessary for the assignment. The supervisor was negligent in assigning the work without providing appropriate protection. The refusal of the work assignment ironically protected both the employees and the organization. Think carefully about safety if there is any possibility of an unsafe assignment.

When employees refuse reasonable work orders—and most assignments are reasonable—insubordination is a serious problem. It is considered to be misconduct and needs immediate attention in the form of discipline. Of course, the severity of the discipline needs to fit the action.

Do you have a textbook that you have kept as a management reference book? I do, and I refer to it often for the purpose of grounding my decisions and evaluation process. I use *Fundamentals of Human Resource Management* by Raymond A Noe, et al., as my reference guide. It contains sections on all aspects of HR leadership, and I use this material in my human capital classes. Every textbook that describes a process for problem correction includes a section on progressive and corrective disciplinary action.

Your options are:

- Verbal warning: Verbal discussion identifying performance deficiencies with expectations for correction
- Written warning: Written documentation providing a record of every discussion concerning discipline
- Suspension: Interruption of active work for the purpose of removing the employee from the workplace immediately (usually unpaid time)
- Disciplinary layoff: Designated time off without pay for disciplinary purposes

Joe the Uncooperative

You were under the gun. The boss needed the month-end data, pronto. Your administrative assistant, Joe, had the month-end figures on his computer but was working on his own expense report, due that day. When you asked him to give you the figures, Joe told you he was busy with his expense report and would get with you later. You wondered, *Who is the boss?*

Stunned, you collected yourself and repeated your request with more detail about the boss's request. Joe was unaffected, repeating that he would get the information to you later, after he'd finished his work. You responded, "This is a direct work order. You need to get me that information now and do your report later." Joe continued to ignore you.

The boss needs information; Joe has it. Joe is not cooperating. Is he having a bad day? It doesn't matter. Think about progressive discipline; do you want to go through the steps of disciplinary action or is this refusal over the top?

Of course, you must fit the disciplinary action to the event. Remember the progressive discipline steps? You must consider the severity of the event, matching the appropriate discipline to the action. Your choices are verbal warning, written warning, final warning, written warning with disciplinary layoff, or immediate termination. A disciplinary layoff ranges from the remainder of an employee's shift to whatever time meets the situation.

Should an employee exhibit gross misconduct, such as an assault, gross insubordination, theft, or threats, the employee should be suspended immediately (after notification to your employee relations department, if applicable). A suspension is an interruption of active employment pending review and extent of discipline. It is intended to remove the employee from the workplace due to the severity of the incident and to permit a thorough investigation. The response to these types of cases is usually termination or a disciplinary layoff.

Examples of employee misconduct include negligence on the job, insubordination, theft and misappropriation of property, making personal long-distance phone calls, and unexcused absenteeism. Incidents of misconduct should be handled at any time during the year in *close proximity* to the event. You should not wait for the performance appraisal to correct incidents of misconduct.

Determine Appropriate Discipline:

- Investigate thoroughly.
- Consider validity of employee's explanation. Is it reasonable?
- Consult your supervisor/manager and human resource representative (this is generally required for time-off discipline).
- Consider employee's length of service and past record of discipline.
- Consider departmental policies and past practices, and be consistent.

Supervisor's Reality Check:

- Employee had notice of possible consequences of their actions.
- The rule is reasonable.
- There was proper and fair investigation into the problem.
- There is proof of the problem (evidence).
- Employees have been treated equitably for similar problems.
- The disciplinary action was fair.

Relevant Questions to Consider

Do you know your organization's policy on disciplinary action? Do you understand the difference between handling misconduct cases and inability cases? How do you know the difference? Do you ask yourself why this problem is occurring? Do you consider aggravating and mitigating circumstances? How would you expect to be treated if you were being disciplined?

____

____

____

____

____

Chapter 13

Handling Discrimination

Joe the Conniver

Joe and his coworker transferred into the same department on the same day. The two employees were of the same race. They were union members who had the seniority to transfer together, but were marginal performers, who had individually been disciplined and were known as troublemakers.

As soon as they transferred to the department, they established a dislike for their supervisor, Joan. They mocked her, ignored her directions, and were frequently missing from the workplace at the same time.

One day, Joan held a staff meeting to describe a new process. Everyone in the department was there and participated. After the meeting, Joe and the other new employee stayed behind and told Joan that they refused to change. The department from which they'd transferred didn't do things that way. After thinking about their resistance, she decided that everyone needed to comply with the change, and she would not make an exception for them.

Things got worse. The employees complained incessantly and were missing in action frequently. Joan knew that she had to discipline the two employees but she was worried about retribution. She needed to move forward with the process, as the work in the department was suffering.

That day, a coworker of the employees was doing her job when they started complaining. The coworker said, "What's with you people? It's pretty nice around here. What are you complaining about?" Joan met with Joe and his colleague separately concerning the absenteeism and insubordinate behavior. They both walked off the job and filed a discrimination suit. They won their case because of the comments of the coworker.

Remember, you must set the tone of no tolerance for discriminatory language. If you observe them, nip them in the bud. But be advised: even though you do not condone these types of behaviors, your organization may be liable for the inappropriate comments of employees.

Joe the Doughnut Muncher

Joe was African-American, forty years old, and obese. He had struggled to lose weight for many years, due to the advice of his doctor and a host of documented health problems. He worked for a university and supervised a crew of temporary student employees who lacked sensitivity and class. They made fun of Joe's weight, drew cartoons of him, and called him "the doughnut muncher." The students got the best of Joe, and he reported the problem to his boss, claiming the students were discriminating against him. The boss told Joe to take care of the problem himself, saying, "But remember the students go to school here—they are our customers."

The students continued to harass Joe, and he suffered in silence.

Joe was in three protected classes: age, race, and disability. His boss had an obligation to take care of the discrimination, regardless of the students' customer status. Joe was harassed in his workplace with no solution immediately available.

Joe discussed the problem with HR, and it was remedied. HR met with the students and told them their treatment of Joe would not be tolerated. They stopped. The fact that they were customers of the organization had not been a factor.

Discriminatory treatment can come in many forms. You have an obligation to maintain a work environment free of discrimination. In this case, the manager was not the defendant. He was in the position to take action to correct the problem. Your organization could be liable for discrimination between employees and customers as well. Make sure policies, standards, and expectations are well communicated.

Joe the Seasoned Employee

"You're old," the new department head said to his secretary, Joe. The newly hired administrator was meeting and greeting his new staff when he insulted the well-respected, long-term employee. His intention was to tease Joe, but Joe didn't take it that way. The boss said that Joe was oversensitive. Joe retired shortly thereafter, years earlier than expected. He filed a claim of age discrimination, but it was cancelled. This resulted in a buyout and release of claims.

Relevant Questions to Consider

What is your approach to handling discrimination claims? Do you know your institutional policies concerning discrimination? Make sure you and your employees understand your institutional philosophy and policy concerning complaints of this type. Review your policy, communicate your process for investigation, and assure compliance.

____

____

____

____

____

Chapter 14

The Most Common Workplace Problems

Joe the Occasional Employee

The boss claimed, "Joe is a great employee—*when he's here*." I wish I had a nickel for every time I have heard that. How can Joe be a great employee if he has an attendance problem?

Managers are generally reluctant to deal with attendance issues. Mostly, they claim they don't want to ask personal questions related to attendance problems and are afraid of any related legal issues.

Coworkers are watching. They know when you don't correct attendance problems. They are the ones who have to pick up the slack when colleagues are missing from work. Confidentiality rules when you are dealing with attendance problems, but coworkers know. People talk, watercoolers exist. If employees think a colleague is getting away with something, they will too. Have you heard "If Joe can do it, I will too"? Don't create bad apples that will spread the problem. Set clear expectations regarding attendance and follow your rules.

Joe was absent intermittently for two weeks. He was gone more than he was present. Coworkers were curious and concerned, and his boss was ignorant about his medical woes. Month-end reporting was imminent. What is a boss to do? This boss didn't ask Joe any questions when he called in, because he thought it was none of his business.

None of his business? There is a large percentage of managers who believe that employees' illnesses are a private matter. Listen up—it is not only your right, it is your responsibility to inquire as to the diagnosis and the prognosis of an employee's illness. What do you tell your director when he comes knocking, asking where Joe's monthly report is?

Remember, it is not only your legal right to ask for the reason that your employee is calling in sick, it is your responsibility to know the reason and the expected duration of the absence.

As it turned out, Joe had hepatitis. It was discovered when the boss asked him for a doctor's statement. By the time the contagious illness was discovered, Joe's coworkers had been exposed for weeks. The local Department of Health was contacted, and the employees were inoculated, way after the fact.

It is perfectly reasonable to create an attendance policy.

Of course, as a general rule, you don't need all of the nitty-gritty details of an employee's illness. Just the diagnosis and prognosis, please. Workforce planning is an important component of your job, and you need to know an estimate of the duration of your employee's absence. A casual two- or three-day absence may not require much workforce shifting. Longer absences will.

Another reason for you to know the diagnosis and prognosis are your obligations under the Family and Medical Leave Act (FMLA). You are required to provide employees with their rights under this very detailed law. You can be held liable for noncompliance both as an employee of your organization and as an individual.

If employees are absent due to a serious illness as defined by the 1993 act, you are required to notify them in writing that their time off is counted toward their twelve weeks (or twenty-six weeks for military) of eligible time off covered under the FMLA. Without proper notice, employees may receive additional time as covered FMLA time.

Under FMLA, employees who work for public employers, or private employers with at least fifty employees, are entitled to up to twelve weeks of time off per year for a seriously ill family member, a personal serious illness, pregnancy, or the birth or adoption of a child. Employees must have worked for at least twelve months, and worked 1,250 hours during the previous twelve months. During this time off, employees' benefits are protected, and they are eligible to return to their job or to a position with like pay and benefits. (Refer to the Family and Medical Leave Act Fact Sheet for particular compliance issues, which can be found in the bibliography at the back of this book.)

Realize the importance of referring to the FMLA Fact Sheet. This information is intended to provide you with the basics of the act.

Some critical facts concerning your compliance with FMLA include:

- The twelve weeks can be taken intermittently or in one continuous time frame.
- Serious illness is generally a period of incapacity of more than three consecutive calendar days, related to pregnancy or treatment for a chronic serious health condition.
- A family member is defined as a spouse, son, daughter, or parent. Keep in mind that if your organization provides FMLA coverage for domestic partners or others not covered under the federal law, employees don't have to waive their entitlement for the family members covered under the law. In other words, even if an employee takes twelve weeks of FMLA time to care for a domestic partner, they are still entitled to take time off for other family members covered by the act. Military families have additional entitlement under the act. Family members of a member of the armed forces, National Guard, or reserves with a serious

injury or illness are entitled to twenty-six workweeks of unpaid leave time in a twelve-month period.

Relevant Questions to Consider

Do you have attendance standard in your workplace? What is the threshold where you have had enough of attendance problems and move to the discipline process? Do you understand employee rights and your responsibilities under the FMLA?

___

___

___

___

___

Joe the Substance Abuser

Gosh, Joe smells like alcohol. It's probably just his mouthwash, right? Joe gets his work done, but he's having trouble at home. He's usually at work. You think, *I'll give him a break. Yeah, it's probably his mouthwash. Or maybe he was at the bar too late last night?*

You start to notice the odor more frequently. You see him coming to work late, and you thought you saw him snoozing at his desk and in his car at lunchtime. You wonder if you need to confront Joe. Nah, he'll work things out.

Now, Joe's work is suffering and he is missing from the office. You are worried that your month-end figures will suffer. You approach Joe with your concerns, and he denies any problem with alcohol. Gosh, you like the guy. You want to give him a chance to fix what is going on, on his own.

The fact is, Joe needs your help. His alcohol use is affecting his livelihood. At your first observation of the symptoms, you need to start the process to correct Joe's problem. What do you do?

Do not be an enabler. Discuss your observations, and their potential workplace ramifications, with Joe. And be prepared for Joe to deny his problem.

According to the American Council for Drug Education:

- Abusers are ten times more likely to miss work.
- They are 3.6 times more likely to be involved in work accidents.
- They are five times more likely to file a worker's compensation claim.
- They are 33 percent less productive.
- They incur health care costs that are three times higher than the average worker's.

As you can see, Joe's problem becomes your problem.

Know these signs of substance abusers:

- They are often missing from work.
- Their personal hygiene suffers.
- They overreact to criticism.

- Their gait may be unsteady, their speech slurred, and their pupils dilated.

Create and communicate a policy that clearly prohibits substance abuse and includes consequences for violations. Do you need to terminate Joe for his substance abuse? It depends. If he is drinking on the job, he is in serious violation of company policy, and his actions will likely lead to immediate termination. If you can, create a process to get him help. If Joe needs assistance from a professional, arrange for counseling, but only with Joe's cooperation. And yes, counseling and recovery from substance abuse is covered under the Family and Medical Leave Act.

Without his agreement to correct the problem, Joe cannot survive in your workplace. Look at the institutional policies at your workplace and make sure you know how to comply with their standards

Relevant Questions to Consider

Are the standards and expectations clear to your employees concerning substance abuse? Do you need to make your expectations clearer? How?

____

____

____

____

____

Joe the Violent Employee

Joe was having a particularly bad time—arguments at home, car problems, bills piling up. When he got to work late, his supervisor was not happy with him. In fact, Joe was met with a simple "What the hell is wrong with you? You are pitiful! Get to work." All Joe could think about was heading home, getting his gun, and shooting the boss.

"Who does the boss think he is? Where does he get off saying '*you…you…you*'?"

First of all, as a manager, you need to check *your* style. When you have an employee with problems that are affecting his demeanor, focus on the issues, don't judge the whole person. Remember, you are concerned with particular aspects of the work relationship. In Joe's case, his threatening behavior was creating a serious workplace dynamic. You can quickly inflame an employee's anger to a new level without careful treatment.

A good approach is to separate the hostile employee from other employees and discuss the reasons for the problem. In other words, let your employee know that you are concerned about his actions, but you are also interested in helping him succeed.

Manage the person and the escalating situation. I am quite certain that many potentially violent actions have been averted by a manager who skillfully held conversations with employees in distress.

- Focus on the present. Ask "How can I help you now?" This focuses the situation on the present time and gives the employee time to reflect on summarizing his or her concerns. This also gives *you* time to get assistance. Do not discount the person's feelings, give orders, or invade their personal space. Remember, you want to de-escalate the anger.
- Use active listening techniques when communicating with an employee in an escalating situation. We are inclined to respond with anger, but listen with full attention to the individual, make eye contact, ask him or her if there is anything you can help him or her with immediately. Avoid "you" statements. Don't be accusatory; remember, you are attempting to calm the upset person. Validate the person's feelings, saying things such as "I understand you are upset." Restate the concerns, and echo the individual's comments back to him or her. Give the employee his or her personal space.
- Investigate thoroughly. Consider all of the facts and make sure you interview all witnesses to violent events. Be aware that the memory of the witnesses may become fuzzy. There may be a reluctance to discuss their recollection due to fear of retaliation or a desire to not get involved.
- Project calmness and move slowly, use an even tone of voice, and acknowledge that it is okay to vent. Focus on the here and now. Your goal is to bring

down the level of anger so you can resolve the immediate problem.

If you experience a crisis, respond immediately to the behavior. Attempt to isolate the individual and contact your emergency services as soon as possible. In any event, remember, don't be a hero. Your personal safety is paramount. Learn from advice that banks use in a bank robbery: don't fight to keep the money. Be safe.

Since the early nineties, violence in the workplace has been a common concern for all types of managers. Any expert in handling violence agrees that the way to deal with violence in the workplace is a solid, proactive approach which includes three critical components.

- **Develop a clear policy with zero tolerance for violence.** Make sure that you create a workplace culture that sets the clear standard that *any* act of violence will not be tolerated. A policy that I created included the language that it's everyone's responsibility to share in the prevention of violence. Employees are required by policy to report violent and threatening behavior.
- **Educate managers concerning respectful treatment of employees.** Check your style; treat employees with respect. This should be the mantra for leaders to follow. When incidents of violence have been researched, in many cases the boss was accused of

abusive or disrespectful behavior. This is not an excuse for workplace violence, but it is a theme to learn from.

- **Put employees on notice with the consequences of violent behavior.** At the University of Michigan, I presented violence education programs with two experts, the director of the Employee Assistance Program, Tom Waldecker, and Police Captain Jim Smiley. We collaborated based on each of our strengths. Our strong recommendations included the creation of an employee notice, with clear standards and expectations.

The most creative approach to violence prevention I've seen is a poster that was intended for workplace bulletin boards. It read, "You don't say 'hijack' in an airport, and you don't threaten in our workplace. Same response." Your local police agency is more than happy to provide you with proactive assistance. Many police departments provide a community police officer to perform a safety audit. An officer will review your workplace and provide you with suggestions on how to make it a safer environment, including the placement of your desks, recommendations for alarm systems, and proactive methods for communicating during emergencies.

Joe the Abusive Spouse

Chris and her husband Joe have been having marital problems, and it is rumored that there is domestic violence at home. She comes to work distraught, distracted, and occasionally bruised. Chris's coworkers are worried that she will bring their problems to the workplace. Joe has already been calling her at work and driving by the office. It is affecting Chris's performance.

Your inclination is to just bring Chris's problems with productivity to her attention during her performance evaluation. She is a good worker, and you expect that Chris will correct the problems. You told her coworkers that Chris's home life is none of your business. Think again. It is your responsibility to maintain a safe work environment. The employees are concerned about Chris's safety and their own. They know that Joe has a history of violence and owns weapons. You don't want to get between Chris and Joe—or do you? What do you do? You have already talked to Chris, and she doesn't want any help. You can't solve her problem, but you *can* recognize both the assistance that she may need *and* your concerns about protecting your workplace.

In this case, the manager convinced Chris to get counseling through the employee assistance program. Chris provided a photo of Joe to keep at the reception desk for purposes of protection and notice. The concerned employees were assured that they were supported by the company's plans for quick action should Joe show up at the workplace. They created an access code to enter the department. The potential for a critical violent incident was lessened, and the workplace was safer.

Startling statistics from the American Institute on Domestic Violence:

- Approximately 75 percent of battered women are harassed at work by their husbands. While this is not only a problem with women at work, 85 to 95 percent of all domestic violence victims are female.
- Homicide has risen to become the leading cause of death for women at work.
- Domestic violence is the leading cause of injury to women.

Yes, domestic violence becomes your problem as a manager and employer. Are you ready for a potentially violent situation in your workplace? Examine your policies, education, and readiness. It will pay off in the event of a violent act in your workplace. Communication is the key to effective prevention for any type of violence.

Remember, when there is violence in the workplace, first and foremost, protect yourself.

Relevant Questions to Consider

How prepared is your workplace to handle an incident of workplace violence? Have you performed a workplace violence audit in your workplace? Do you set a clear expectation with a zero tolerance for violence? How would you communicate to your employees about the standard?

____

____

____

____

____

Joe the Jokester

Joe was a perpetual jokester and slacker in the maintenance shop. He liked to threaten the staff that he would get them if they told the boss about his antics. When his coworkers complained about him "going too far" with his comments and gestures, his boss said, "Oh that's just Joe." Just Joe? He was creating a work environment that some considered hostile.

Remember, his boss was aware of the problems with Joe. One day, Joe told a coworker, Jim, "I'm going to kick your ass after work in the middle of the street, where no one can touch you." Jim told his boss he'd had enough of Joe's harassment and wouldn't take it anymore. He wasn't joking. He was afraid that Joe would attack him outside of the workplace.

The boss had not discussed Joe's behavior problems with Joe, believing it to be idle shop talk. *After all*, he thought, *Joe won't do anything. He's a jokester.*

After work, in the middle of the street, Joe made good on his threat and attacked Jim. Holy smokes. The boss had known Joe had been threatening coworkers and he hadn't taken it seriously. Is he liable? You bet he is.

Jim was fine, with the exception of a few bruises. The boss was lucky that Jim was a good sport and a fine worker. Joe was fired. Did it matter that the attack happened on public property as opposed to company property? No, actually. This attack spilled out of the workplace and onto public property. If there is a workplace connection, it is likely that the company is liable. Jim could have filed suit, claiming that the company was liable due to lack of protection of the employees.

This is called negligent retention. The boss knew about a problem with Joe and chose not to address the issues. Joe should have been warned about his inappropriate behavior. Joe possibly could have been saved as an employee if he had realized the seriousness of his actions. In that case, at least the boss would have been able to prove that he had warned Joe about the consequences of his behavior.

Relevant Questions to Consider

Have you neglected to solve a workplace problem or have you observed a manager ignoring a problem? Did the problem fester and escalate? Think about the potential ramifications of waiting too long to take corrective action.

____

____

____

____

____

Joe the Con Artist

Joe was hired as a clerk in the accounting department. The boss, Cheryl, did her job right, checking his references and his criminal record since he would be handling sensitive financial information. Joe's record came back clean.

After a couple of months, Cheryl became suspicious of Joe's activities. He was commonly away from his desk, and when he was there, Joe was frequently on the phone. She started to look at Joe's work more carefully.

One day, Joe was away from his desk when his coworker Judie took a message from his sister. The message was, "Ask Bruce to call me. It's important." Judie told her there was no Bruce working there. The sister said, "Oh, yes there is. Bruce is my brother's nickname."

Bruce? Joe? Cheryl needed to look into this. Of course, when she asked Joe about the phone call, he confirmed that was what his family called him. Having handled his paperwork, Cheryl knew there was no "Bruce" in his name. Was this a case of identity fraud? Oh, yes.

Cheryl called HR, and an investigation was started. HR and the local police agency traced his background and discovered that Joe had taken on the identity of a well-respected fund manager at a major financial institution. His real identity was that of a former felon who had been convicted of a white-collar crime. There was a fox in the financial henhouse!

Obviously, Cheryl's job was to remove him from the workplace as soon as possible. If Joe became aware of the department's knowledge of his true identity, he could possibly falsify records or steal from the organization. He had the tools and has already proven to have significant credibility problems. There was no progressive discipline here. The only option was to get him out.

Of course, the real Joe was notified of the identity theft.

Relevant Questions to Consider

Do you check employment references for your new employees? How about a criminal record check? Since falsification of records is a serious problem, how would you handle this problem in your workplace?

____

____

____

____

____

Chapter 15

"Out-boarding" Employees

Joe the Unrecognized Manager

Joe was a well-respected manager, but he was angry. He felt that he was not permitted to perform his job without constant scrutiny. He gave his two weeks' notice and intended to spend the notice period grooming his staff to take over his responsibilities. The next day, however, his boss told him, "I think it's time for you to go." He was escorted off the premises without the ability to say a fond farewell to his colleagues. Now, this was a very popular, fine employee. He thought, *Why am I getting the bum's rush? Are they going to think I was fired? What, no cake?*

The way an employee is treated on his or her way out the door—out-boarding—is as important as a good on-boarding process—really. When it is time to say good-bye, whether the separation is voluntary or involuntary, helping employees to leave with dignity is a critical step that prevents claims and lawsuits against the organization.

If employees resign and are shown the door with an escort and a Bankers Box filled with their personal belongings, their final impression of the organization will be compromised. We have all seen this in the media: the snapshot of employees leaving a company with their heads down and a few belongings in hand. What do you think is on someone's mind at that moment of his career? It surely isn't a warm feeling about the employer. Their shame or embarrassment will quite likely lead them to think about times when the employment experience was not so favorable, and they may consider legal counsel.

Keep in mind that there are circumstances, such as revealing proprietary interests, stealing customers, and breaching confidentiality, that warrant immediate removal. These circumstances are specific to business concerns; the everyday situation should not be handled in this mode.

Let's talk about some protection techniques. Arrange for a going-away gathering. Realize the value of a cake. Yes, something as simple as a cake could save you thousands of dollars. The good wishes of colleagues and administrators may have a lasting impact on the departing employee. If those negative thoughts dissipate, any extra effort is worth the time and expense.

Think about conducting exit interviews. Of course, there are mixed reviews on the value of a survey upon termination, but you may learn valuable information that can help you to manage your employees. Take this information with the proverbial grain of salt, but look for trends that can help you. If valued employees are leaving your organization, sit up and listen. You want to know why.

Relevant Questions to Consider

How does your organization outboard employees? Do you have farewell gatherings to wish employees well? Do you have an exit interview process? If so, review your questions to insure that you are gathering information relevant to your workplace.

____

____

____

____

____

Separation Agreements

If an employment separation is on shaky ground, such as denial of a promotion, unreliable witnesses to an event that lead to a termination, or a sense of disparate treatment, a separation agreement is a good way to create a clean termination.

A separation agreement includes a few key elements. The introductory paragraph sets the tone of the agreement with some important, but not too detailed, facts concerning the critical event or ongoing problem that led to termination.

The terms of the agreement need to be carefully communicated in the second paragraph, using phrasing such as, "You, Joe, will receive $10,000 on or around June 30. Should a reference be requested from an outside company, only your dates of employment and position will be verified. You are not eligible for reemployment with the company."

The final paragraph is eminently important. You need a full and complete release of all claims to your company. There will be no contest or claim concerning your employment relationship. The agreement must be acknowledged by the employee and an authorizing representative of the institution.

If the employee is age forty or over, you must provide him or her an opportunity to consider the terms of the agreement for twenty-one days, and seven days to revoke the agreement if the employee chooses to do so. When you are creating a binding agreement, always work with your Human Resource office or an attorney to assure compliance with your institutional policies and laws. (See Appendix B for settlement agreement language.)

Last Chance Agreements (LCA)

Sometimes, you are just not ready to call it quits with an employee who has a troubled employment history. You may have all or most of the information necessary to sever the employment relationship, but you would like to provide the employee with a final opportunity to correct the problem.

By doing this, you may be turning on the switch that is necessary to create a good employee.

If you choose to provide an employee with an LCA, you benefit from an agreement/acknowledgement signed by the employee, acknowledging that there is a problem that he or she will attempt to correct. This is the essential function of an LCA.

Similar to the settlement agreement, you must set the stage for the agreement. Provide the details of the problem and discuss the ramifications for violating the LCA. Demonstrate the steps that you have taken to notify the employee of the problem, such as corrective discipline, and inform them of the consequences of failing to correct the problem. The plan needs to be clear and complete, e.g., "You must correct your problems with performance. It is a requirement that you audit at least seventy invoices per day with accuracy. We will provide you with the assistance of your team leader to relieve a portion of your workload for the next week."

Don't lock yourself in to a date, such as, "I will give you three months to correct this problem." The employee may drag his feet for two months and try to correct the problem at the eleventh hour. Instead, make it clear to the employee that he must correct the problem immediately. If you have pearls of wisdom to assist in the correction, please list your ideas in the document, but be brief.

Set review dates, but leave it open for you to be the decision maker. Include language such as "We will have ongoing discussions for review of your progress. We will discuss your progress on a weekly basis for purposes of mutual feedback." This leaves the length of the time frame of correction up to you. (Refer to Appendix C for a sample Last Chance Agreement.)

Chapter 16

The Bully or Management Terrorist

Joe the Terrorized

Remember when your parents said, "Sticks and stones may break my bones, but words will never hurt me"? Maybe we are a more sensitive society today, but that just ain't true anymore, at least in the workplace. Startling statistics underscore the severity of this serious workplace problem.

According to 2007 statistics from the Workplace Bullying Institute, 37 percent of American workers have been bullied at work.

It's sad but true: management terrorism, in the form of bullying, is alive and well in the workplace. Can you legally bully employees? In a sense, yes; bad management is not illegal. Of course, if you add a touch of discrimination of a protected class into the mix, you're treading on dangerous ground. In this case, you will get yourself in legal trouble. But in general, bullying in and of itself does not get you in legal hot water.

Joe the Bullied

Workplace bullying first became abundantly clear to me in one memorable grievance hearing. Joe the custodian filed a grievance because his supervisor was allegedly verbally abusing him. He explained in his grievance hearing that despite the fact that he was risking his "macho image," he couldn't take the abuse any longer and had to report his concerns. Joe said that his supervisor, Kurt, bullied him by regularly yelling at him in the presence of his customers, using expletives, and verbally attacking him. This is a perfect example of the bullying personality. While Kurt was still in my office, I questioned him about the allegations. Kurt said he did not understand why Joe had made such claims, and that they were unfounded.

When it was time for them to return to work after our meeting, Kurt went down the hall to tell Joe that he would transport him to his workplace. Unaware that I was observing his behavior, Kurt immediately began to yell at and berate Joe. When I approached Kurt and told him that he was demonstrating the very behavior described to me in the grievance hearing, he again said that the claims were unfounded; he did not know what I was talking about. This type of behavior was such an integral part of Kurt's personality that he did not even realize he was verbally abusing the custodian, or at least he would not admit it.

We all know Kurt the bully. His type is found in many, if not most, workplaces. Word spreads fast about the bully at the watercooler, and eventually employees keep their distance.

Remember this: you must *not* permit the bullies of the workplace world to continue abusive behavior. Management bullying is a serious disease that can seriously affect your workplace and become a huge problem. Bullying hurts performance, and fosters anxiety and depression. What are you supposed to do? Well it's not an easy issue to handle, but it needs to be corrected carefully and with clear consequences.

Stand your ground, and tell him or her that you won't tolerate the bullying any longer.

Quite likely, the bully doesn't realize that he or she is being abusive. If the bully is one of your employees, you need to take charge and minimize the effects of the behavior on the workplace. When speaking with the office bully, focus on the particulars of the problem behavior; be specific, and explain simply and directly the consequences of failure to correct the problem. Listen carefully to the bully's explanation. There could be an underlying explanation that has merit, but there is never an excuse for aggressive and abusive behavior. If the employee needs assistance to correct the behaviors, provide an employee assistance program or other support through conflict resolution processes.

Don't let the problem fester. It will likely not go away by itself. You may be inheriting serious workplace morale problems if you don't nip the bullying behavior in the bud.

First of all, the workplace terrorist will have followers. Yes, bullying is very contagious. Of course, we all understand the concept of cliques at work; that starts early in childhood while kids are choosing teams. I have seen many employees singled out in the workplace because one of the members of the clique has convinced others that they should follow suit and harass a coworker. This often results in unwanted turnover, which is costly to your organization, not to mention the possibility of harassment claims.

According to Dr. Gary Namie, Director of the Workplace Bullying Institute, and author of *The Bully at Work: What You Can Do to Stop the Hurt and Reclaim Your Dignity on the Job,* the top ten bullying tactics are: [1]

1. Blame for "errors"
2. Unreasonable job demands
3. Criticism of ability
4. Inconsistent compliance with rules
5. Threatens job loss
6. Insults and put-downs
7. Discounting/denial of accomplishments

1. Gary Namie and Ruth Namie, *The Bully at Work: What You Can Do to Stop the Hurt and Reclaim Your Dignity on the Job* (Napersville, IL: Sourcebooks, Inc., 2003), 27.

8. Exclusion, "icing out"
9. Yelling, screaming
10. Stealing credit

Clearly communicate the standards concerning workplace decorum. Make sure your staff understands the consequences of unacceptable behaviors toward colleagues—and make sure you stop these behaviors swiftly.

Remember this: bullying behavior that is excused will continue, will likely become a workplace standard, and can possibly be looked at as a badge of honor. It's not how loud you talk; it's the content and strength of the message.

But what happens if the bully is your boss?

If your boss is a workplace terrorist, it is likely that you are a victim, at least some of the time. Your boss will usually spread out the abuse. He or she may exhibit abusive behavior toward you one day and move on to another person the next day. You and your colleagues will be left wondering who's next. Occasionally the bullying boss will fixate on one particular employee most of the time and will only occasionally move on to another.

One manager changed her bullying behavior by occasionally taking a breather for a day or so. "She probably took her meds today," the employees joked as they enjoyed a reprieve. If the sad reality of an abusive boss is a mental health concern, information needs to be carefully and clearly brought to the attention of senior leadership before it affects the employment status of reputable staff. The bullying boss will quite likely poison the reputation of subordinates to higher levels of leadership while destroying the employment relationship of the victim(s).

You need to handle the bullying done by someone in a senior position in a manner similar to how you handle this behavior by a subordinate. You need the facts. If you have a high comfort level and know the boss very well, then by all means discuss the issue to give him or her a heads-up. If you choose to go up the ladder to report abusive behavior, you *must* have clear and complete information. This could be difficult for you professionally, and it may backfire. You need to decide how important the issues are to you. Be aware that bullies are usually highly respected for their aggressiveness. If you complain about a bully, you will usually be the one who loses. Proceed with caution.

Take comfort in the fact that bullies often do each other in. They spend most of their time trying to cover their tracks.

Bad managers often hold their employees "hostage" with the threat of discontinuing employment. At times, upper management turns a blind eye to this behavior if they are getting the results they want. In this case, you need to decide whether you can continue in this employment relationship, appeal, or quit.

If you are the boss, this behavior cannot be condoned at any time or in any place, period. Don't permit abuse in your area of control. This can result in allegations of a hostile work environment, and negligence in your workplace can be costly, in the form of turnover, claims, and appeals.

Relevant Questions to Consider

Think about your workplace. Are there bullying behaviors that are occurring? Are you permitting bullies to terrorize your employees? Look at policies or standards that you can put into place that will prevent the effects of this behavior.

____

____

____

____

____

Chapter 17

Employee Appeals

Joe the Powerless

Joe is a friend of his HR department. He has been having problems with his boss Kate for some time, and goes to the HR department to strategize ways to work things out with her. "Why can't we just get along?" he moaned. "Kate is crazy!"

You see, the boss has an open-door policy, right? But there is no appeal process. Joe has a whole host of complaints—very legitimate concerns—but he thinks there is no one listening. Trying to get an appointment with someone up the chain of command was impossible. HR was powerless in this case; senior management didn't care. Joe's only choice was to try to let things slide and get along.

Joe was a diamond in the rough, but Kate would never experience the depth of his skills; he eventually quit because upper management wouldn't listen to him. Kate *was* the problem.

Appeal processes or grievances are not only for unionized staff. In fact, from my perspective, they belong in every organization in some form. Think of it this way: Do you want to look at a problem "inside the tent or outside the tent"? Do you want to know when there are problems bubbling in your workplace? Remember, a complaint is a gift. It will permit you to have the first opportunity to evaluate a problem and see if there's something you can fix yourself.

Wouldn't you rather handle the problem instead of having a lawyer or outside agency investigate the issues? Some organizations shy away from an appeal process due to potential liability concerns. The reality is, if there is a problem that employees are passionate about, it will likely make it to the top leadership in some fashion. Believe me, liability usually does not go away, even if you don't know about it.

An appeal process can be as simple as "another look," a process I developed for an employer who had no formal grievance process. Provide a basic statement in your employee handbook or on your employee web site or intranet that charts out a simple process to discuss a problem. It can look like this: "Go to your immediate supervisor. If that does not solve the issue, discuss the problem with the next in the line of management."

A discussion at any step of the way with your human resources manager is encouraged. Remember, the HR department in most organizations provides a problem-solving arm, and its mission is to help managers accomplish their goals. Get to know them; it's best to have had discussions with your HR staff prior to investigation of a serious problem.

Relevant Questions to Consider

Does your organization have an appeals process? How do you handle employee complaints and concerns? Do you personally have an open-door policy, and are employees comfortable discussing problems with you?

____

____

____

____

____

Chapter 18

Management Types to Avoid

I'm sure you have observed behavior that is counterproductive and unbecoming of a manager. I certainly have. The result is often the loss of a good employee.

Think about your reputation as a problem solver or compassionate manager. When you are ready to move up the career ladder, situations like those that follow can ruin your reputation. Remember, leadership is always watching. Don't be that guy or gal.

Joe the Wicked Boss of the West

Joe flew down the hall like the Wicked Witch of the West with the hired consultant in tow. "Where is the directors' salary information?" he demanded of his good employee. Joe had not previously asked for the information and was met with a look of confusion. To save face with the consultant, he made the employee his scapegoat, berating and blaming him. Dazed and on the verge of tears, the good employee said, "Jeez, I need another job," and soon quit. Joe lost a good worker.

Joe the Wedding Crasher

Joe announced his engagement to his fellow employees and to his boss. His wedding was being planned almost one year in advance. The couple had won a honeymoon trip and there was fanfare in the newspapers. The boss said, "I have no problem with you taking the time off."

Enter Joe's boss's supervisor. She said to Joe's boss, "Who are *you* to give him the time off from work? Our policy says you have to give time off strictly with seniority. He is one of our newest employees. He can get married on one of two dates; make him choose one of them and change his plans."

The stunned employee took the problem to the very top of the organization to keep his wedding date. He was a well-respected worker who was prepared to quit over the challenge. This led to a reconsideration of the manager's judgment. Her rigidity and inability to use creative problem solving damaged her reputation. Joe quit, and the manager said, "That was my management right." Because of Joe's resignation, the wedding went on as scheduled, but the manager's reasoning skills and reputation were questioned by senior leadership, and a good worker was lost.

Joe the Relocated New Hire

For planning purposes, when Sherry the director hired Joe as a new manager, she asked him if he needed time off in the next few months. Joe explained that he needed to return to his home state to retrieve his belongings. He was told there would be no problem with the trip.

When the time came to schedule his move, Sherry informed Joe that granting his time off was contingent upon the absences of other managers and the completion of his projects. Remember, this is a new manager who had moved to a new state, as well as learned a new job.

Joe could not travel to retrieve his belongings because Sherry could not arrange for him to be away from the workplace. This was not a good, honorable start to Joe's employment relationship. Joe found another job.

Joe the Copier

June was Joe's boss at the Copy Center. She gave Joe a warning for not charging his buddy the standard price to make a copy. June did the right thing. She restated the standard and told Joe that if he violated the policy again, he would likely be fired. He did it again. June scheduled a meeting to discuss Joe's termination.

In response, Joe called HR to report that June gave her son a free pass to make copies. Was this information relevant to Joe's case? Joe was clearly warned of the consequences of violating the Copy Center's policies and violated them again anyway.

HR laughed off the allegation. They thought the story about June's son just couldn't be true. After all, she was planning to fire Joe. When HR asked June about her son, she said, "Sure, I let him use the copier. Don't managers get perks?"

Managers may get perks, but not when employees get fired for the same thing. In the end, Joe was not fired, and was instead reminded once again of the policies. June learned an important management lesson and was warned of the consequences of future bad judgment.

Joe the Victim of Plagiarism

Joe's boss Jane came knocking. Jane announced that she was writing a book and asked him for some procedures he'd written and training materials he had created. Jane wanted to use the material in her book and assured him that she would reference his work. Joe excitedly and proudly provided the information. *Wow,* he thought, *people will be able to be Google me!* Jane eventually published her book and failed to provide Joe with the proper reference and recognition, leaving him in the dust.

What's an employee to do? If Joe complained to Jane's boss, he would risk serious retaliation. After all, he liked his job and didn't want to jeopardize his career. Joe just suffered in silence. Joe lost respect for Jane, and so did his coworkers. Remember, the grapevine is a powerful communication tool.

Many of us are fearful that the success of our staff takes away from the luster of our leadership. Have you witnessed a boss taking credit for a work product that was clearly not his work? Or maybe it was your work? In reality, you earn your stripes as a boss based upon the work your staff performs.

Relevant Questions to Consider

Think about exceptional work that has been performed by your staff. What chances have you let get away that you could have recognized? How have you been left in the dust?

____

____

____

____

____

Talking Turkey about Management Style

Let's talk turkey. Take a close look at your own management style. My students in management classes look at the preceding examples and are appalled at the lack of solid management practice. They ask, "Where are these bad bosses and why are they permitted to manage people?" Reality tells us that they are all around. Some organizations sanction and encourage this type of behavior.

The choice of how you manage employees is yours. You can make solid decisions about your management style and choose to treat employees with respect—or not. The result of your choice will probably dictate your future success in business. If your style is similar to that of the bad leaders described above, you will hit the proverbial brick wall at some point in your career.

Ten Types of Managers to Avoid

Managers who don't follow the Golden Rule.

Okay, so you hear this everywhere, but it's so important. Mistreatment of staff by berating, yelling, and otherwise publicly demoralizing them is the single biggest demotivating factor in managing people. Always reprimand and correct problems in private. Once coworkers observe a reprimand, it is very difficult for an employee to turn around a problem. Follow a twenty-four-hour rule. Remember when your kid's coach or teacher asked parents to wait twenty-four hours to discuss a problem? The same principle applies; don't react in anger. If the problem is so significant that you need to remove an employee from the workplace immediately, suspend him or her, collect your thoughts as you look at all the circumstances, and then act on the case. Remember, based upon "equitable" treatment, each case is different.

Managers who don't know how to make a decision and bring work progress to a screeching halt.

Stagnation is a workplace disease. Hoping that a problem will go away works some of the time, but not all of the time. I have observed countless times when problems have spiraled out of control because they have been permitted to silently grow. Of course, every issue that is brought to your attention is not a major problem for correction, but choose your battles wisely and make sure that you address the issues with the most impact on your workplace.

Managers who take credit for work that is performed by someone else.

First of all, managers look stronger because of the work and success of their staff. Think of a time that you or a colleague experienced pangs of frustration when a manager paraded work accomplished by you as their own. It's a large morale killer and can occasionally be downright illegal.

Managers who try to make others look bad to make themselves look better.

A manager frequently contacted the leadership team to report on the failures of her staff. She would contact the team using the phrase "Cleanup on Aisle Five" in her correspondence to denote the fact that she had to micromanage the situation to correct the problem. The root cause of the problem was irrelevant at that point. The leadership was aware of the problem and had a tainted view of the situation, regardless of the reason. All too commonly, managers throw employees under the proverbial bus to make themselves look better.

Managers who show favoritism (most of the time).

Favoritism is the mistreatment of staff due to irrelevant factors, such as race, sex, etc., and it can be a career-stopping concern. Treat all employees with respect. Employees notice.

But, when one of the wisest managers I know was asked why there was a perception of favoritism in his department, his response was simple. "Yes, I favor some of my staff, and what's the problem with that?" Favoritism has many faces. The reason this wise guy was comfortable with favoritism was that he favored movers and shakers, the dedicated staff who were learning, applying knowledge, and eagerly taking on new challenges. There is a difference between favoritism and recognizing the best of your staff. That is good management of people.

Managers who are set in their ways and will not acknowledge fresh ideas.

I love this theme; it reminds me of a favorite movie of mine, *Going My Way*. In the film, a young priest with fresh ideas comes to St. Mary's Church to join a seasoned expert. The old priest is irritated by the young priest's new ideas and teaching techniques, and takes his cause to the archdiocese. Much to his surprise, the old priest learns that the higher-ups in the church placed the young priest in charge *because of* his fresh ideas.

Be careful about resistance to new ideas. Don't take a wholesale approach of denial. It will make you appear uncooperative to the ever-changing work environment. There are many great ideas to be considered that can make everyone's reputation soar.

Managers who will not give constructive feedback and surprise employees at review time.

There should be *no* surprises at evaluation time. Remember, employees wait for critical feedback to know what and how to improve. Provide both positive and negative comments throughout the year. Keep a running list of accomplishments for ease in evaluating employees; thorough notes lead to clear communication, as well as more respect from your staff.

Managers who ignore problems, hoping they will go away.

Some problems will certainly go away, but you need to effectively pick your battles. Remember, employees wait with bated breath to see how well you will handle problems in your workplace—and it will be discussed in the grapevine.

Managers who accept nepotism or personal relationships in the workplace.

Yes, those managers are out there, and the rest of us are watching. Nepotism goes hand in hand with preferential treatment. I never recommend that employees in a personal relationship have a supervisor/subordinate relationship as well. Take a look at your policies. Make sure that you clearly communicate the rules. Should this mean that no one can have a personal relationship in the workplace? Not necessarily. You just need clear communication and to make sure employees understand that a relationship must be disclosed to senior leadership. A boss in a personal relationship should not have the final control over evaluations or salary increases.

Managers who are snakes in the grass.

They are out there, and they are watching others. We have all seen them slithering to the boss. They betray colleagues by using information against them to benefit themselves. Managers need to be forthright in their observations and communication.

Chapter 19

Questions about Documentation

Managers ask many questions about documents and what to do with them. This chapter provides a general guide.

Where should files be kept?

Any type of personnel file should be maintained in a secure location, e.g., a locked file cabinet, locked desk, or locked office.

What is a supervisor's working file?

A supervisor's working file is typically a folder that is kept in a locked drawer or office that contains notes with day-to-day observations about the performance of a particular employee.

Can electronic information be considered part of the personnel file?

Information that is maintained on a supervisor's computer is considered part of the supervisor's working file. This includes e-mail exchanges related to actions against an employee. This information is discoverable in a legal action.

How long should information be kept in a current employee's file?

Information should always remain in a current employee's record. The company needs a whole picture of the person's employment history.

Do you document verbal warnings?

While a verbal warning is exactly that, a verbal exchange with an employee that discusses a problem with some aspect of employment, it is recommended that the supervisor make note of the conversation and the issues discussed. This information can be maintained in the supervisor's working file in the form of an e-mail, handwritten note, or memo.

How long should information be kept in files after termination?

It is recommended that information be kept for at least seven years following an employee's termination. This information provides a historical look at performance. There are very few exceptions to this rule.

Should your personnel department purge employee files that are centrally maintained?

Yes, after seven years following termination. If an employee was not recommended for rehire, the information should be kept in some other format, likely on microfiche.

What do I do with the employment records if someone transfers out of my department?

Keep the records. You may be asked for information concerning the former employee by the other department or HR. You may be asked to forward attendance records or disciplinary information when an employee transfers.

What should not be kept in a personnel file? (Applies to HR and departmental files.)

- Medical information must be kept in a *separate* locked file.
- Casual notes regarding day-to-day performance issues should not be kept in a department or personnel file.
- Employee references supplied to another employer.
- Materials that refer to more than one employee.
- Information relating to a criminal investigation.
- Grievance records.
- Information regarding an employee's political activities.

Can employees appeal information contained in a personnel file that is kept by HR or the department?

Yes, employees can appeal information in a personnel file. This can be handled informally or through a formal process. Alternatively, the employee can place a letter of rebuttal in the file.

What about positive documentation or commendation letters—do they hurt us when there is discipline?

Tough question. Should an employee receive good performance evaluations and commendation letters, this could mitigate a case of discipline. Even when an employee receives salary increases that are consistent with satisfactory performance standards, the discipline case can be mitigated. If there is a peer-nominated recognition program, this information is of limited value from the standpoint of performance of the employee.

Can employees see their own personnel files?

Yes, federal law states that employees can review their own files. This includes the file kept in HR and the departmental record, but doesn't include the supervisor's working file. They can, however, be limited to two annual requests. There is no specific time frame following the request, but it must be a reasonable time period. They can request copies of their information for a modest copying fee.

How/when/why are union staff records treated differently?

Some labor agreements have language that addresses the retention of letters of discipline. For example, an AFSCME Agreement at the University of Michigan states in paragraph 287b, "In taking disciplinary action, the University shall not take into account any prior incidents which occurred more than two (2) years previously." This is standard negotiated language that is included in most collective bargaining agreements. This does not apply to employees who don't belong to unions. This does not mean that documents should be removed from records. They remain as history. However, the discipline that is older than two years should not be considered.

How long should we keep application materials for job candidates?

Your records concerning jobs that were posted and filled should be retained in the departmental records for a minimum of three years. This includes résumés, copies of bid forms, and notes concerning your selection process.

Records of Disciplinary Action that Support the Facts

Your disgruntled employee goes to your boss, claiming absolute unfairness on your part. You have been recording incidents of tardiness and unexcused absenteeism by this employee for months, and have provided him with appropriate feedback. You have the details and the documents, and are confident you can successfully defend the claim.

Think about what the boss would say if you didn't have the details to back up your concerns. New and seasoned managers want to know how to handle problems, how to discipline employees. When the time comes—and it will—you want to have this information at your fingertips.

Here's how to simply prepare documentation that will not only provide rationale for disciplinary discussions, but also give you peace of mind.

- When a supervisor gives a verbal warning, he or she should keep a record of the discussion. Verbal warnings are just that: verbal. A record of the discussion belongs in the supervisor's working file, not in the formal personnel file.
- Should a written warning or documentation of a more serious form of discipline be necessary, information should be communicated as simply as possible. Refer to Appendix A for simple template instructions to follow when administering written discipline.

A written warning provides formal documentation of a problem or deficiencies in the workplace, and letters of discipline belong in the personnel file. It solidifies the fact that this is a serious problem that must be corrected in order for the employee to remain employed.

The warning should have a serious tone. The problem should be identified clearly and succinctly, and should set the expectation that more discipline will follow should the employee fail to correct (not just lessen) the problem.

A wise labor attorney I worked with, the late Bill Lemmer of the University of Michigan, always advised getting the point across enough for the employee to understand the problem and stop. Make sure you tell them the consequences of failure to correct the problem. Do not provide more information than is necessary.

Don't include compliments in a documentation of disciplinary action. A common mistake that supervisors make is to say "You are an excellent employee, but…" or "I regret that I have to do this, but…" Don't send mixed messages. Keep in mind that when you must discipline employees, it is *all* about the problem at hand and potential for correction. The time for accolades is in a performance review and in commendations.

Relevant Questions to Consider

Look at your recordkeeping practices; do you properly maintain employee records and protect yourself? Are you prepared for employee challenges? Perform your own audit of your records and make sure you are able to defend your facts.

____

____

____

____

____

Chapter 20

Old Dogs, New Tricks, and New Approaches

Joe the Has-Been

Bob managed a staff of call center computer specialists who fixed computer problems. Joe was one of his employees. The staff often told Bob, "Don't send Joe to fix my computer. He doesn't know what he's doing."

"Oh no!" Bob cried. "Joe is my senior technician! What am I going to do?"

The first question Bob needed to consider was: "*What* doesn't he know and *why*?" Joe had been a well-respected technician, but suddenly he couldn't please anyone anymore. Was this a fairness issue, an age-discrimination problem, or a training problem?

The answer was that Joe didn't keep current with his profession. Despite the fact that he was given every opportunity to participate in state-of-the-art training and was notified of updates, Joe did not maintain his competencies. He was planning to retire in a couple of years and didn't think it was necessary. The result? Joe was not allowed to work for a couple more years. He lost his job. His response? "You can't teach an old dog new tricks."

"Stayin' alive" is critical to your profession. Particularly in professions related to information technology, human resources, law, and medicine, you must show your knowledge of state-of-the art processes and new developments to remain effective in your job. Read trade journals and seek out the latest in technology for your field.

It is heartbreaking to terminate an employee at the end of his career because of neglect of knowledge. As the boss, it is your job to ask about an employee's expertise in their job and seek out any reluctance to learn new tricks. Look for alternative job assignments if that position no longer fits the employee's capabilities.

I have handled a few of these cases. They can be upsetting. With pre-planning, however, many jobs can be saved in our fast-paced work environment.

Chapter 21

Office Romance

So, I married my coworker. Thirty years ago, that is, and we're still ticking. My husband and I worked in different departments, and everyone knew about our relationship. There were no policies against workplace dating at that time, but that was also the time of the three-martini lunch.

What about office romances? Do we really want to limit the love bug? According to a 2004 survey by *Glamour* magazine and Lawyers.com, 41 percent of American workers between the ages of twenty-five and forty have had an office romance.[1] However, dating at work means potential liability for you and your company, so it is up to your organization to determine the level of tolerance for such relationships.

1. Lawyers.com, "Interoffice Romance Survey," news release, August 12, 2004, http://research.lawyers.com/Interoffice-Romance-Survey.html.

Do you want to take on that liability? One organization that I have worked with took a strong position on personal relationship liability. They created a policy that stated that no one in the capacity of managing people was permitted to have a personal relationship with *anyone* in the organization. Can they do that? Sure. Is this type of policy wrought with problems? Absolutely. This is management overkill. A potential policy revision would be: "Managers should not foster or maintain personal relationships with employees in their area of management."

Joe the Social Director

Take a look at the company superstar and director, Joe, who enjoys his after-work cocktails. A few too many drinks may result in a loss of his desire or ability to follow corporate policy concerning dating employees. Are you willing to enforce your policy because of one Friday night screwup? After all, he is one of your top employees. Keep in mind that you need to follow your policy consistently. Be reasonable with your expectations.

Create a firm and clear policy about romantic workplace relationships and distribute your expectations widely. Take time at staff meetings to discuss the policy and review case examples. Don't forget to create a safe way for employees to report workplace sexual concerns, such as a complaint process specific to relationships. Remember, keep the workplace complaints "inside the tent" if you can. You want an opportunity to correct the problem before it spirals out of control.

Relevant Questions to Consider

Think about whether or not you are or would be willing to allow romantic relationships in the workplace. What are the parameters of your policy? How would you administer violations and possible exceptions to the rule?

____

____

____

____

____

Chapter 22

Use Your Resources and Pick Your Battles

Joe the Independent

Joe was a first-rate tutor. Everyone went to him for his special expertise. Joe aspired to bigger and better things. His goal was to become the second-in-charge of his division. With his sterling reputation, he believed he would surely reach his goal. However, while he excelled in his field, he knew very little about leading a division.

Joe eventually got his chance. His dream job became available. Despite the fact that Joe didn't have director-level experience, he got the job. He was given his chance to be noticed and shine.

Enter Joe's reluctance to ask for assistance. He made it clear that he wanted to handle his staff based on his good instincts. He immediately ran into some rather complex issues. I was Joe's management consultant when he contacted me to discuss the problems, and I encouraged him to make sure he was tapping any available resource to do the job well. He insisted that asking questions and involving outside experts would be a sign of weakness.

Don't ever forget: asking for assistance is not a sign of weakness; it is a sign that you know how to solve problems using any resource you have available.

Well, Joe was not successful using his instincts alone. He failed as a director because of ungrounded decisions. Joe next went to a new director job outside of the company, not learning from his experience. Joe is once again in a staff position, no longer leading.

The 80-20 Rule, or Pareto's Principle

Do you trivialize problems in your workplace? Or do you take issue with everything that crosses your desk? Look at the issues that have come your way and see where you may want to spend more of your time and effort.

Of all of the useful management principles, I am particularly fond of the 80-20 rule, and I have used it repeatedly in many difficult situations. This rule states that 20 percent of the problems in your workplace are vital issues for attention, and 80 percent are trivial issues. Also, 80 percent of your time is generally concentrated on 20 percent of the work. If all of your time is spent on issues that are not critical to the business, you must be a weary person. Concentrate your efforts on what really matters. Much of the rest can go by the wayside.

Okay, again, how many *bad* bosses have you observed? Chances are those bosses never learned this rule of the "vital few and trivial many." I know one boss who made a point of always attacking each situation. Employees scattered when the boss entered the department. Believe me, employees know when an attack is about to start.

Chapter 23

Grim (and True) Tales of Management

Joe the Toy Store Manager

The toy store was bustling during the busy Christmas season where I was picking up one last Christmas toy for my son. The manager was obviously disturbed at the slow speed of a teenage temporary worker. He charged at the temp, berating her and calling her names because she was inexperienced with the holiday rush. This was all in front of a line of shoppers.

The employee, obviously panicked by this treatment, fumbled and could not continue the transaction. The uncomfortable observers started discussing the problem—not the slow teenager, but the bad manager. More than one shopper left the store without purchases, claiming that they would not support a store that mistreated employees.

Never, but never, admonish employees in public. It can ruin your reputation and your business. Make conversations meaningful and conduct them in private.

Relevant Questions to Consider

What are your standards for bringing problems to the attention of your employees? What would you change?

____

____

____

____

____

Joe the Dog Groomer

A large chain pet store has a grooming salon on the premises. While dropping off my dog for her haircut, I observed the manager stop the groomers from doing their work to make a spectacle of one employee in front of coworkers and customers. The manager pointed her finger at the employee and yelled, "You, there. Get over here. All the rest of you, listen now…" She continued to bark orders to the staff while the customers looked on. I wondered, *Is she going to talk to my dog that way?*

"How do these people treat our dogs if that's the way they treat their employees, and our dogs can't tell us what they do to them?" remarked one of the customers. I left the store and found a new groomer. Don't lose business by barking at your staff.

Relevant Questions to Consider

How would you handle a supervisor who treats employees in this manner? Communicate expected behavioral norms to your employees and assure compliance. Are you willing to lose valuable customers who witness this type of behavior by your supervisors?

____

____

____

____

____

Joe the Fast Food Cook

Often, restaurant chains will empower a teen to manage the front of the house at their restaurants. Usually, the young supervisor is a good food service worker, but not a good manager. I witnessed this firsthand when I placed my order with a young woman who, just a few seconds before, had been very curt with her staff about their lack of knowledge in burger flipping. Obviously, she forgot that I was the customer and addressed me with the same bad attitude. When I asked her what the problem was, she stopped being nasty with me, but continued to "broil" her employees.

Don't tolerate bad behavior by your staff just to save a buck; you could potentially alienate a customer. Don't get me wrong; teens can manage, but they need to follow the rules of a respectful workplace like all other managers. If they don't, it's your liability.

Joe the Flight Attendant

My husband and I were frustrated by our travel experience. The airline had lost our luggage, a flight was cancelled, and we were weary. Finally, we took our seats in the plane and got ready for the final leg of our trip. We were lucky: the third seat in our row was vacant and the plane door was shut, meaning no more passengers to occupy our row. We could spread out and comfortably snooze!

All of a sudden, here came Joe, the customer-service-savvy flight attendant. Two trendy travelers wanted to change seats and asked him if a single traveler could move into the empty seat next to us, leaving his prime seat for them. There was no compelling reason behind their request, like to take care of their kids, parents, etc.

Hey! What happened to my plan for comfort? The single traveler felt guilty saying no, and we felt guilty telling him no. So, the trendy travelers swooped up the prime seats at his and our expense. The single traveler sat down next to me. He was hot—not the handsome kind, but with a fever. *Oh great,* I thought at the time. *Now I'll probably catch the swine flu or something!* I stewed the entire flight, upset at the inconvenience that Joe the Flight Attendant caused.

Similar to giving a new pack of crayons to one student while the other students use remnants, prime customer service for one customer can upset your other loyal customers.

Relevant Questions to Consider

Look at your customer service philosophy. Is it communicated effectively? Have you accommodated some at the expense of others?

____

____

____

____

____

Chapter 24

Mantras for Managers

These are common sense items that you already know, but they're worth a reminder to get you through the day:

- This is a job, not your life.
- Treat your workplace like your house. Keep it neat and full of good people.
- Don't let your job take priority over your kids. In fact, bring them in to visit and make them a part of your work life.
- Eat light during the day. Don't let food make you sluggish.
- Eat breakfast. Yes statistics show that breakfast jump starts your brain and makes you sharper.
- Get up and walk around every couple of hours; it keeps your blood flowing and clears your mind. And

for heaven's sake, make sure you take a walk around the block when you feel angry.

- Work two half days instead of one long one. Do something for yourself midday such as a walk, stretch break, or snack.
- Drink water.
- Keep up to date on current events; you'll be more interesting and will be able to make more small talk with your colleagues.
- Listen to your favorite music—with headphones. It helps pass the time and relax you.
- Socialize with your colleagues, but not too much. Don't let your colleagues overpower your relationships with your family.
- Don't play the role of bullpen catcher too long. You want to get into the show. Look for a new team where you can shine.
- Remember: a workplace is like a family unit. Most of us spend more time communicating with our coworkers than our families. It's truly and sadly so. But remember, even though some employees may feel like family, they are your coworkers first and foremost. Your job is to manage your staff. When the employment relationship is over, only the truly good friendships endure, and some employers prohibit future contact with former employees.

Chapter 25

Good Guidance

Joe the Exceptional

Joe did an exceptional job leading his staff and proudly presented the year-end report. You have never seen such a fine, complete job. Without Joe, you would not have reached your financial goals or, most importantly, looked good in the eyes of the president. An all-staff meeting was scheduled to announce the unexpectedly excellent results. The president praised you, and a loud, appreciative applause erupted. You quickly acknowledged Joe as the driving force for the report's success. Did it weaken you? No. Did it lessen the impact of your success? No. Did it create a reason for Joe to try even harder next time? Of course it did.

When you commend Joe, make it short and simple, and do it as close to the event as possible. You don't want to lose the momentum. Focus specifically on what he did particularly well. This is not the time for general performance evaluation. Copy God and everybody. Make his exceptional performance a big deal.

Mimi Rules

My mother, Mimi, was loved by all and had a gift for knowing how to make you feel good about yourself. The term "Mimi" is a fine acronym for recognition. It stands for:

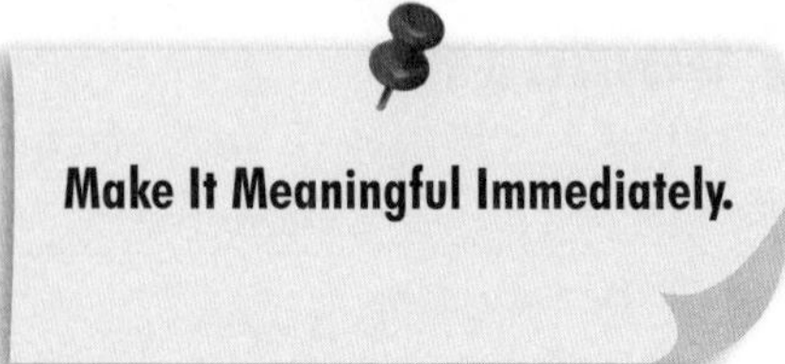

When you observe exceptional behavior, don't let the opportunity get away to fuss over your employees. Holy smokes, you want to encourage others to say, "I want to be noticed, too!"

Speaking of Moms: "Momisms"

Treat people right. (The most important advice of all.)

Think about the best boss you've ever had and the worst boss you've ever had. I bet the best boss treated employees the way they want to be treated. I've seen the best of them and the worst of them. The worst boss I ever had was a true micromanager in every sense of the word. She complimented work and in the next sentence trashed the same job. Managers were reluctant to go to her for assistance because of her negative demeanor.

Pick yourself up, dust yourself off, and start all over again.

Life is about learning and starting over.

You will make bad decisions; you *will* stub your toe—we all have.

You will want to give up on occasion, but remember those experiences make you who you are.

Take an aspirin for your headache.

Don't let aches and pains affect your performance. And go to work; most of the time, you *can* get up and go.

Don't communicate bad news to employees when you don't feel well.

Make sure that you get yourself under control before you tackle problems.

If it's not nice, don't say it—at least publicly.

Conversations about problems must be in private to be effective. Of course we all know that in the life of a manager, there will be times when unpleasant information must be communicated. Hold discussions thoughtfully and truthfully.

If I jumped off a cliff, would you follow?

Think carefully about who you choose to emulate. Many people fall off that cliff.

Don't follow the crowd.

Be an individual with your own ideas; learn from others but think for yourself.

Look for the silver lining.

There is a reason for everything. Have you ever thought, *Why me?* Think about the situation you're in, learn from it or let it go.

Count your blessings.

We tend to focus on the negatives in our workplaces. There is a reason why you landed where you are; focus on your strengths. If the negatives outweigh the blessings, think about a change.

Dress for success.

Look to the work environment for cues on how to dress. You don't want to blend into the wallpaper, but you do want to look sharp and appropriate.

Deal with it, let it go, and move on.

"My boss said I am like a dog with a pork chop." Don't chew on it long after the meat is gone.

As the old Chinese proverb says, "Give a man a fish; you have fed him for a day. Teach a man to fish and you have fed him for a lifetime." According to my colleague, Bridget O'Connor, "Just give me the damn fish!"

And of course, keep a good relationship with your parents and call them; they have a wealth of good advice and you're lucky to have them! Don't forget: the older your children get, the smarter you become.

Chapter 26

Be Prepared for Potential Challenges

Protect Yourself

I couldn't believe my ears when I heard the administrator lie under oath. Blatantly, flat-out lie to a judge, so help me God. Yes, she committed perjury. We've all seen what happens to people who lie under oath. It ain't pretty. Whether or not you agree that Martha Stewart or a whole host of athletes lied in front of a grand jury, they have sorely paid a price for their indiscretions.

Always be prepared for your workplace decisions to be challenged. It is a crossover from your professional to your personal life. When questioned about the facts of a case, don't use the phrase "I don't remember." It weakens you and diminishes your credibility. Remember, you are in charge of the livelihood of your staff.

Your company is likely to have an indemnification policy that will provide legal counsel if you or the organization are sued. It is very common for a complainant in an employment suit to not only sue the organization, but you as well. Your company will support you *if* you have done an honest and honorable job. If the organization does not believe you or support you, you may not be entitled to the use of their lawyers.

This is why you always need to be prepared for challenges. It is not common to be sued over your decisions in regard to treatment of employees, but always think about doing the right thing and use your resources. Make sure you treat others the way you would like to be treated. Go up the chain and get support when you have an issue. Be complete in your investigation of problems, and involve your employee in the process of problem correction.

You never know when you may be challenged on your decisions. I hope that you will have few to none of these challenges. By being a good boss, your chances of prevailing are significantly improved. By the way, the boss who perjured herself is no longer employed. She paid the price for her indiscretion.

Remember: revisit your policies and standards. Were they clear to your employees or were violations honest errors in judgment? Ask yourself, was the employee the right hire for the job? Was he truthful about his qualifications? Was the employee given a good start to his employment? Was orientation and grooming done to your liking? Think about your employee's entire record; has he been treated equitably, considering all of the circumstances? Did you keep good records and evidence to be used in the case of a challenge? Did you get support from your leadership, and did you use your resources? Did you think about laws that may affect your decisions?

These challenges may come in the form of:

- Grievances
- Labor arbitration
- Outside agency complaints
- Unemployment compensation claims
- Claims of discrimination with the U.S. Equal Employment Opportunity Commission (EEOC)
- Requests under Right to Know Act
- Requests to review employment records permitted by the Freedom of Information Act (FOIA)
- Unfair labor practice claims filed with the U.S. Department of Labor
- Other civil or criminal actions

If you are challenged, relax. You are a good boss who can defend your actions. You will be prepared.

Chances are your organization has a good support system and resources that you can work with when you must take an employment action or receive a challenge. Nonetheless, it is important that you have a working knowledge of laws related to managing people. As more than one legal contact has advised, ignorance of the law is no defense.

Take a look at the resources and web sites listed under "Recommended Web Sites and Readings" at the back of this book. Have this information at your fingertips. Do a reality check. Make sure you understand the basics of employment law. There are many law firms that host legal updates to advise on changes in laws that affect managers. The legal updates are an invaluable resource and are reasonably priced as well.

A great no-cost source for policy or practice information is any public university web site. Information on these sites is public knowledge and fully accessible. Universities conduct considerable research and create their policies based upon the best practices out there. Check them out. They can save you much time and effort, and provide you with stunning work.

Chapter 27

Advice from Some of the Best

We've all heard that teachers learn more than their students. The same thing applies to management consulting. In the stage of research, information gathering, and benchmarking, the consultant is always in a learning mode. I have had the pleasure of experiencing the roles of both consultant and teacher, and have retained the rich experiences of each discipline.

The fun part is retaining the experiences and thoughts of those we value. I use them when future decisions are necessary. I have asked some of those individuals who have grounded my experiences for an answer to the question "What makes a great manager?" You will see that people from very different backgrounds have very similar thoughts.

Start keeping your own "Advice from Some of the Best" list. You may be surprised by the guidance it will give you.

Judy Roper, Retired HR Manager, Ross School of Business, University of Michigan

A great manager needs to have vision *and* leadership. Someone who listens, has compassion, can articulate the direction the ship is heading, and gives suggestions to not only her or his direct reports, but is comfortable enough to speak to, listen to, and tell everyone how they might help get the ship to the right port. Identify certain people in a crowd and say, "Suzie, you could…." And work the room. This shows everyone that not only do you know their names, but in some ways you know what people do. Of course, we wouldn't expect you to know about everyone, but even just a few gives the impression that you know more about them. Perceptions are key. So leadership, vision, listening, and compassion are key. People like great leaders; history has proven that, and then they will follow.

Dan Andoloro, Former Business Student

What makes a good leader? I truly believe that to be a good leader, an individual needs to possess the following skills. A good leader needs to be a good communicator. You need to be able to convey your ideas and vision, whether it is verbal or written, to your team in a method which provides a clear direction. A successful leader also needs to be a good listener. A good leader needs to be open to the ideas of others. Next, a good leader needs to be a team player. He needs to be confident in his ability and not worried that someone in a lower position may outshine him. Good leaders develop good people, not hold them down. Lastly, a good leader needs to be a **good motivator**. He needs to understand the strengths and weaknesses of his team members. When he understands each team member as an individual, he then knows what is important to each one, as well as what it takes to motivate that person. What may work with one person might not be the same method that will work with another.

Bridget O'Connor, Recruiting Goddess and Former President of BKO Enterprises

Good leaders know that it's all about the people to be successful. It's that simple: "respect everyone 365."

Bruce Pringle, Retired Director of Staff Human Resources, University of Michigan

I hire good people, and their performance makes me stronger. Many leaders are afraid of good performers who will outshine the boss. It's just the opposite—the good performers make you look like a better leader.

Robin Kabat, Associate HR Director, Florida Atlantic University

A good manager has to create an atmosphere where employees are encouraged to be creative and are not afraid to make mistakes. A good manager has vision and is able to inspire employees to share in that vision and work to accomplish its success. A good manager is a leader, which means that someone wants to follow. A good manager encourages employees to think on their own and builds a foundation of trust so that employees feel empowered. A good manager knows and understands the mission and goals of the employer and understands that everyone plays a role in successfully accomplishing those goals.

Joe Roberson, Retired Athletic Director, University of Michigan

Mostly as a result of my experience in athletics, I learned that leadership is based on convincing people to follow your lead, not frightening them with intimidation.

Bob Moenart, Retired Controller, University of Michigan

Treat everyone fairly. Those who perform the best will be rewarded. Support your leadership staff in their decision making as long as those decisions were thought out and made sense based on the facts at the time. If you treat people fairly and support them in their roles, they will perform at their best. I look at employees that go beyond their day-to-day responsibilities in the performance of their jobs as the future leaders in the organization. I expect all staff will adhere to ethical standards in their relationships with others and the community they serve.

Robert Powell, Financial Manager

The sign of a great leader is being a great listener.

Cheryl Kern, Billing Manager, Océ Financial Services, Inc.

Honestly, ask the person who actually does the job how to make it better.

Tina Zuccaro, Pediatric Nurse Practitioner

Get right in and do what you do. Someone who wants to be a boss needs to boss, not just be called a boss.

Zack "Tanner" Siegal, Eleven-Year-Old Future Leader

Treat people with respect, be caring, follow the Golden Rule, treat others like you like to be treated, with courtesy, and be trustworthy. *(Author's note: Yes, he is eleven years old.)*

Dave Siegal, Accountant and Director of Payroll

Treat the top person the same way you treat the receptionist or mail person. Any way you slice it, we're all part of the company.

Rebecca Murphy, Eleven-Year-Old Future Stetson Scholar

A nice boss follows rules but isn't mean and rude.

Steven Solitto, Eleven Year Old

A boss needs to give you time off to do things you like to do, like play football.

Sherry Pedigo, Medical Office Manager

A great boss makes the workplace a fun place to go.

Fred Ferreira, Former Vice President of the New York Yankees, the Montreal Expos, and the Florida Marlins, and Sports Agent

Communication is very important. Everybody is different—handle situations individually. There are certain ways to get your point across. Build relationships; it makes managing easier.

Kate Elliott, Medical Nurse Case Manager for Thirty Years

A good manager leads people rather than manages them. He or she leads by example, with a good work ethic, focus, and people skills. One of the most important traits in a good manager is a sense of humor—you cannot take yourself too seriously. Your employees are your most important asset, and you are not more important than they are!

José Velez, MBA Student

In today's ever-changing marketplace, there are three main actions that will lead a good manager toward success: coach, motivate, and develop.

Ron Chambers, Petrol Station Owner, Gold Coast, Australia

Get managers to the point where they can be independent with good systems and guidelines. In my absence, I can know that my business will be okay.

Marie Paen, Publix Store Cashier, Boynton Beach, Florida

You can tell a good manager by the way they present themselves in front of customers.

Maizie Blue Powell, Eleven-Year-Old Family Dog

From my experience, yes, you can teach an old dog new tricks—if the dog wants the treat bad enough!

Jim Smiley, Retired Police Captain, University of Michigan

A good leader can excite and engage his team. He or she involves them in the forming of a plan as well as the execution. A good leader knows that when the team "owns" the project, there is a greater chance of success. A good leader is accountable, respected, knowledgeable, and always shares the glory, along with the responsibility. A good leader will be fair, consistent, and value all team members in that manner.

Tom Waldecker, Director, Faculty and Staff Assistance Program, University of Michigan

An effective leader in an organization is foremost one who is able to communicate well. The first and foremost part of any communication is the ability to listen first and then show acknowledgment of hearing those who work with you. The ability to motivate and set a positive tone within one's work group is also an essential element for a leader. Demonstrating a tone that is receptive to new ideas and allowing staff and colleagues to propose ideas and take risks are essential elements in a dynamic workforce. The best leaders in my career have been good leaders who took the time to hear what I had to say. Even when they ultimately did not agree with my input, they took my thoughts and ideas into consideration.

Glenn Mack, President of Le Cordon Bleu College of Culinary Arts Atlanta

A great manager sees the value that every employee brings to an organization and is able to match individual skills and interests with company goals.

Terry Powell, Director of Strategic Accounts and Customer Care, Océ Financial Services, Inc.

A great manager controls the highs and the lows of each business day. Do your best to be a mentor for your coworkers. Respect on the job is not easily earned, so work hard, lead by example, and make yourself accessible to the people around you to help their daily challenges. Be open to change as your coworkers have good ideas (just because it has always been done that way does not mean that it is the best approach). Acknowledge your employees for their contributions, and never take credit for their accomplishments. You will receive your successes through management of their initiatives.

Karen Costner Milazzo, Owner of Curves, Boynton Beach, Florida

As a manager, I find it is very important to listen. Some of the best ideas will come from the people who work for you. It is even more important to recognize and reward them for their ideas. I have found that some consider a management position a position of control, and those who *do* have less control than they know.

Phil Vera, Collections Supervisor, Océ Financial Services, Inc.

Managing people is easy if you know how to recognize each individual's talent level. The difficult but exciting part of managing each individual is developing that individual's talent. Motivating that individual through teaching and encouragement creates a confidence within that individual to perform at a higher level that not only contributes to the individual's growth and the growth of the manager, but to the overall growth and success of the company.

Michael Stevenson, Senior Associate Athletic Director, University of Michigan

You can't please everybody. Don't let criticism worry you.

John Contrino, Technology Sales Executive, Chicago, Illinois

I communicate our goals and objectives; then I listen. I don't have hidden agendas.

Larry F. Steele, Director of Mutual Funds, Saint Clair Shores, Michigan

Hire good people and pay them competitive wages. Watch good workers, especially ones that want to move up the ladder, and don't be afraid to reward good workers.

Chapter 28

Know When to Hold 'em, Know When to Fold 'em

You are in charge of your career destiny; you will know when you are in the right job to make it your career. You will also know when it's time to change. You may not want to listen to that inner voice, but take it seriously. Look at the reasons for your desire to change and consider your potential options.

Joe stopped in to say hello and good-bye. He had gone up the chain of command to complain about his boss to no avail in the politically charged environment. His boss was brutal, unreasonable, and an outright bully. Joe had to decide whether the possibility of searching for a new job in a tough job market was worth the benefits of less stress and better self-esteem. It was to him. He loved his job as a director of human resources but realized that reducing his high blood pressure was more important than keeping the job that caused it. Joe had worked his way up to this job but decided that his health was more important than his career achievements. Joe resigned his position, leaving behind the effects of an irrational boss.

Many of us don't have the same option as Joe, or at least we don't think we do. You choose where you are in your career. If you decide to stay at your company to grow your retirement, to enjoy your relative freedom in your spare time, or out of a lack of motivation to do anything else, then you have made your choice. None of these options are bad; they're just reasons to do a reality check about where you are in your career.

My father gave me some of his sage advice at the start of my career. I had moved around from employer to employer, trying to find my niche, when he said, "You need to get seniority. That's what it is all about." You see, my father was from a generation who thrived with seniority; it had its serious value from the standpoint of promotions, benefits, and pensions. Many of us fall into our career choices based on where we are in the here and now. Some of us look up twenty years later and think it's too late to seek out what makes us satisfied in our careers. Think again numerous times in your career.

I didn't move around again but stayed in my position in human resources for twenty-three years, but not without self-probing thoughts about other careers. In fact, people change jobs an average of ten times between the ages of eighteen and thirty-eight, with a commonly known turnover roughly every three to five years early in the career. I found my niche where I thrived, and I thrived in human resources and loved every minute of consulting with the fine managers I had the pleasure of working with.

Remember: look within yourself to decide what is the right career and place for you. Set your goals and follow your course.

I'd found my niche. That is until a downturn in the Michigan economy drove my family out of Michigan into Florida. The toll of the downturn and the move was significant for me, because it reminded me of the value of my career, to concentrate on the important things in life, and of the importance of job security and making money.

My husband Terry, my son Ryan, and I tried the commuter family routine where we traveled between three different states; Terry worked in Florida, Ryan was in college in Maryland, and I was working in Michigan. We realized after three years that the cost was too significant, both financially and emotionally.

Many professionals successfully manage the commuter family arrangement. It can work, but from my experience, not for the long run. Juggling family life is tough enough without the added challenges of commuter careers. Once I made this decision, my family became my primary focus. I left the comfort zone of my career. Sad but true: my family had been taking a backseat to my career. I adjusted my priorities and had to build a new life.

Only you will know the right niche for yourself. Sage advice is relative and dependent on the economic climate, generational norms, and your personal goals. I left the career I love, and I'm now making my way in a new state, cutting my teeth in a new environment, and starting over. I wonder what my father would say about my latest choices. No matter what path you take, remember to enjoy your adventure.

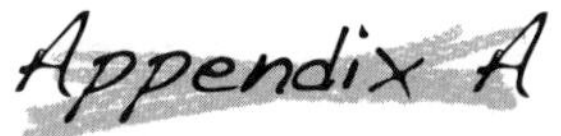

Written Warning

To: Joe
From: The first-line supervisor
Re: Misconduct

You were given a verbal warning on January 5, 2004, for unexcused absenteeism. Since that time, you have incurred six additional incidents of unexcused absenteeism. A summary of your unexcused absences follows:

January 10: Ten minutes tardy
January 31: Extended your break by fifteen minutes
February 10: Eight minutes tardy
February 14: Fifteen minutes tardy
February 26: Eight-hour absence; no call, no show
March 25: Ten minutes tardy

This record demonstrates that you have failed to correct your ongoing problem with attendance.

Your failure to correct your misconduct will result in further disciplinary action up to and including discharge. *(Author's Note: This phrase is important in order to document your action and set the expectation of what will follow should the employee not correct the problem. It is a serious action and your monitoring and follow-up is important for assistance in correcting the problem.)*

Cc: Personnel File
The boss's supervisor
HR Manager

Appendix B

Settlement Agreement

Settlement Agreement
By and between The Corner Brewery and Joe

This confirms the agreement reached between Joe and The Corner Brewery regarding his employment status. The following terms set forth a full and final settlement of all claims:

- Mr. Joe will resign from his position at The Corner Brewery on (Date:__________)

- Mr. Joe will receive a check in the amount of $10,000.00, less withholdings, on or around January 20, 2010. He will also be paid for his unused vacation accrual in his final paycheck for time worked.

- The Corner Brewery and Mr. Joe agree that the terms of this agreement will be confidential and will not be released to third parties except as required by statute, court, or governmental authority.

In exchange for considerations outlined above, Mr. Joe agrees to release The Corner Brewery, its agents and employees, from any and all claims Mr. Joe, his agents, representatives, or successors may have, including any claims under the Age Discrimination in Employment Act, and all other claims arising out of or in connection with his employment or retirement from The Corner Brewery, which may have occurred prior to the date on which this Release of All Claims is executed.

Mr. Joe acknowledges that before signing this Agreement, he has read it and fully understands its terms, content, and effect, and that he has been advised in writing to consult an attorney of his choosing and has relied fully on his own judgment in its execution.

Mr. Joe acknowledges that he has been given at least twenty-one days to consider this agreement (unless he chooses to sign the Agreement prior to the twenty-one-day period, and in that case, he waives the remainder of this period). He may revoke it within seven days after signing it, if he chooses to do so.

____________________Date:____________________
Mr. Joe

____________________Date:____________________
The boss

____________________Date:____________________
HR Manager or legal representative

Appendix C

Last Chance Agreement

Last Chance Agreement
By and between Joe and Acme Toy Company

This Last Chance Agreement confirms the parties' recent discussions resulting from the Disciplinary Review Conference (DRC) held regarding Mr. Joe's continuous record of unexcused absenteeism. The following are the terms under which Mr. Joe's employment will be maintained.

Mr. Joe will be given a five-day disciplinary layoff (Dates:_____________), and there will be no grievance or other appeal of this disciplinary layoff.

The parties understand and agree that any future misconduct will result in Mr. Joe's discharge.

This Agreement is without prejudice or precedent to any action that the Acme Toy Company may have taken in the past or may take in the future under similar circumstances.

Should Mr. Joe violate the terms of this Agreement, he understands and recognizes that he will be discharged without the convening of a DRC or access to the grievance process. The terms of this Agreement will remain in effect for twelve months from the date of signing.

Mr. Joe acknowledges that before signing this Last Chance Agreement, he has had the opportunity to seek any legal counsel of his choosing, and that he has relied fully upon his own judgment in executing this agreement.

Accepted and agreed:

____________________Date:____________________
Mr. Joe

____________________Date:____________________
The boss

____________________Date:____________________
HR Manager or legal representative

Cc: Personnel file
Departmental record

Bibliography

American Institute on Domestic Violence. "Domestic Violence in the Workplace Statistics." http://www.aidv-usa.com/Statistics.htm.

Blake, Ross. "Employee Retention: What Employee Turnover Really Costs You." Web Pro News. http://www.webpronews.com/expertarticles/2006/07/24/employee-retention-what-employee-turnover-really-costs-your-company.

Lawyers.com. "Interoffice Romance Survey." News release, August 12, 2004. http://research.lawyers.com/Interoffice-Romance-Survey.html.

Kickbully.com. "Field Guide." http://www.kickbully.com/page1a1.html.

Peter, Laurence J., and Raymond Hull. *The Peter Principle: Why Things Always Go Wrong.* New York: HarperCollins, 2009.

University of Michigan Health System. "Management Rights and Responsibilities." http://www.med.umich.edu/umhshr/supervisor/rights-responsibilities.html.

University of Michigan Human Resources. "AFSCME 2005 Contract," art. 20, sec. D. http://hr.umich.edu/staffhr/contracts/AFSCME2005contract.html.

———. "Resources: Flexibility in the Workplace." http://www.hr.umich.edu/compclass/flsa/flexibility.html.

U.S. Bureau of Labor Statistics. "Workers on Flexible and Shift Schedules in May 2004." News release, July 1, 2005. http://www.bls.gov/news.release/pdf/flex.pdf.

U.S. Department of Labor. "FairPay Fact Sheets by Occupation." http://www.dol.gov/esa/whd/regs/compliance/fairpay/fact_occupation.htm.

U.S. Wage and Hour Division, U.S. Department of Labor. "Fact Sheet #28: The Family and Medical Leave Act of 1993." http://www.dol.gov/esa/whd/regs/compliance/whdfs28.pdf.

Recommended Reading and Web Sites

Ferrazzi, Keith. *Who's Got Your Back: The Breakthrough Program to Build Deep, Trusting, Relationships That Create Success and Won't Let You Fail.* New York: Crown Publishing, 2009.

Who's Got Your Back describes a method of mutual support by which three people you choose can transform your life and won't let you fail. They help you set goals and tell you the truth.

Kickbully.com. http:///www.kickbully.com

Check out this great web site, kickbully.com. It provides a full review of workplace bullying behavior. The writers of this field guide to bullying must have known the same bully that I knew. She seriously affected my career and would have yours as well.

Lawyers.com. http://www.research.lawyers.com

From finding a lawyer to sample forms to discussions of legal issues, Lawyers.com provides you with a source to find advice and data concerning your employment issues.

Lancaster, Lynne C., and David Stillman. *When Generations Collide: Who They Are. Why They Clash. How to Solve the Generational Puzzle at Work.* New York: HarperCollins, 2002.

When Generations Collide is a fun analysis and description of the differences between the generations and how they view life differently. Lancaster and Stillman provide excellent advice and methods to help all generations get along in the workplace.

Namie, Gary, and Ruth Namie. *The Bully at Work: What You Can Do to Stop the Hurt and Reclaim Your Dignity on the Job.* Naperville, IL: Sourcebooks, Inc., 2003.

Drs. Gary and Ruth Namie provide stunning information about workplace bullying and recommendations about how to stand up to for yourself and regain your dignity on the job.

Nelson, Bob. 1001 *Ways to Reward Employees.* New York: Workman Publishing Company, Inc., 2005.

Dr. Nelson provides both nontraditional and logical ways to recognize and reward employees. It is an excellent resource.

Noe, Raymond A., John R. Hollenbeck, Barry Gerhart, and Patrick M. Wright. *Human Resource Management: Gaining a Competitive Advantage.* New York: McGraw-Hill Irwin, 2008.

Human Resource Management: Gaining a Competitive Advantage is a good reference book to have at your fingertips for all aspects of managing people.

Stone, Douglas, Bruce M. Patton, and Sheila Heen. *Difficult Conversations: How to Discuss What Matters Most.* New York: Penguin Putnam, Inc., 1999.

This book was written as part of the Harvard Negotiation Project. The authors developed expert advice for difficult conversations with employee issues and negotiations.

WorldatWork. http://www.worldatwork.org

The nonprofit organization WorldatWork is known as the Total Rewards Organization. They sponsor webinars and seminars specifically devoted to attracting and retaining employees.